Developing Critical Professional Practice in Education

Developing Critical Professional Practice in Education

Yvon Appleby and Ruth Pilkington

niace
promoting adult learning

Published by

promoting adult learning

© 2014 National Institute of Adult Continuing Education (England and Wales)
21 De Montfort Street, Leicester, LE1 7GE

Company registration no. 2603322
Charity registration no. 1002775

The National Institute of Adult Continuing Education (NIACE) is an
independent charity which promotes adult learning across England and Wales.
Through its research, development, publications, events, outreach and advocacy
activity, NIACE works to improve the quality and breadth of opportunities
available for all adults so they can benefit from learning throughout their lives.

www.niace.org.uk

For details of all our publications, visit http://shop.niace.org.uk

Cataloguing in Publications Data

A CIP record for this title is available from the British Library

978-1-86201-655-2 (print)
978-1-86201-656-9 (PDF)
978-1-86201-657-6 (ePub)
978-1-86201-658-3 (Kindle)

All websites referenced in this book were correct and accessible at the time of
going to press.

The views expressed in this publication are not necessarily endorsed by the
publisher.

Printed in the UK by Marston Book Services, Abingdon.
Cover design by Book Production Services, London.
Typeset by Avon DataSet Ltd, Bidford on Avon, Warwickshire, UK.

Contents

Figures and tables

Figures

Tables

Contributors

Yvon Appleby

Until recently Yvon Appleby was a senior lecturer in the School of Education and Social Science at the University of Central Lancashire (UCLan). In this role she worked within and across several postgraduate professional development programmes and, whilst mainly based in Preston, designed and delivered courses in further education hubs across the north-west. Much of her work, and interest, lay in connecting further and higher education by making learning opportunities accessible and relevant to a wide range of professional educators. Much of her research and writing has been in this area. Yvon joined UCLan in 2007 from Lancaster University where she was a research fellow in the Lancaster Literacy Research Centre working on several national adult literacy projects. A large amount of her research and writing in both institutions has been in developing collaborative ways of working with colleagues and students and supporting professional networks. She is now a freelance consultant.

Ruth Pilkington

Until 2014 Ruth Pilkington was principal lecturer in professional development and higher education in the School of Education and Social Science at UCLan, which she joined in January 2005. She now works freelance. She began her career as a business linguist, moving to staff and education development as a result of managing two nationally funded projects in the UK. She assumed course leadership of the postgraduate certificate in learning and teaching in higher education at UCLan in 2002 and designed and developed the MEd (professional practice in education) and a professional doctorate (EdD) as progression routes. Ruth has published on the subject of employability and professional development. In her work on professional learning within the higher education sector, she has developed a body of work in the use of dialogic approaches to assessments and on continuing professional development.

Lynne Barnes

Lynne is divisional coordinator for the British Sign Language and Deaf Studies team at UCLan. Brought up in the deaf community, she worked as a teacher of deaf children and as support tutor for post-16 deaf students before setting up the Deaf Studies degree programme in 1993. Lynne also acts as an adviser to deaf and hard of hearing students across the university. Her research interests are in the pedagogy of deaf learners and access for deaf students within higher education. She has organised and contributed papers to numerous conferences, developed a national access course for deaf students and a bespoke British sign language teacher training course and is a consultant on many national and European working groups and projects. Lynne was awarded a National Teaching Fellowship in 2008 for her work in deaf studies and in establishing support services for deaf students in higher education.

Christine Hough

Christine Hough is a lecturer in the School of Education and Social Science at the University of Central Lancashire. She is the module leader for the core modules on the degree programme Children, Schools and Families. Christine's professional background encompasses some 25 years as a teacher in secondary schools (PE and Mathematics) and three years as an Ofsted inspector. From 2002 she worked as an educational consultant for the Secondary Heads Association (now the Association of School and College Leaders) both in the UK and overseas. Since joining UCLan, Christine has developed several projects including one supporting learning and skills in HM prisons and in young offender institutions as well as a suite of resources and a professional development package for training in sexuality awareness.

Acknowledgements

This book is supported by the practices, energies and enthusiasm of many people that we have worked with. We acknowledge the support and interest that we have received from colleagues in our institutions, both personally in our working relations and across the formal and informal networks that we belong to. We owe a huge debt to the students we have worked with who teach and manage in the further and higher education sector. As teaching is an active, and for us collaborative, practice many people have been involved in co-constructing, de-constructing, and developing new professional knowledge. We have talked about it, puzzled over it and shared common understanding and experiences, as well as questioned why things don't always work. Some insights have come directly from the classroom, including curricula which structure learning and teaching, whilst others have emerged through seminars and conferences. These rich and often varied professional educational environments have made us question our assumptions and practices, enabling us to develop our ideas which we share here.

As authors, Yvon and Ruth have benefited from participating in various educational and professional networks, sharing ideas with colleagues, researchers and educational developers. Of particular significance to us is the work of the Higher Education Academy (HEA), the Staff and Education Development Association (SEDA) and the Learning and Skills Research Network (LSRN). In a similar way our chapter collaborators, Lynne and Christine, draw upon their own professional networks in deaf studies and in sexuality training to support their work. For each of us, in different ways, our professional networks have enabled and challenged us to develop as more critical professionals. We acknowledge that this has at times been a challenge in the face of time and energy commitments to our students and colleagues. Making time and space for our professional development, with colleagues and in networks, is not always easy for us, but it is essential in renewing our energy, in finding new ways forward and in learning from others. In other words it inspires and energises and is something we value.

Introduction

The aims of the book

This book collects together our ideas, experiences and vision for supporting critical professional development in education. These are things that individually and collectively we have developed over many years and want to share with others. We don't assume that we have a universal blueprint, or even that we have everything right, but in the true spirit of learning we offer this for others to develop, amend or critique. We are aware that we are writing at a particularly turbulent time in further and higher education in the UK, shaping our work in what is termed a post-1992, or 'new', university in the north west of England. Our geographical location and local student profiles will therefore be different from others in the UK and in European or international settings. Some of what we discuss has developed from our particular working environment and geographical location. However, it is also common to the field of education, nationally and internationally, as we face similar threats from the continual erosion in working conditions, professional autonomy and an increase in target-driven performance cultures. Another commonality, we hope, is the aspiration to deliver high-quality learning based upon continuing professional development as teachers, educational developers and managers.

We realise that there is a difficult and delicate balance to achieve between realistically acknowledging what is negative in our current situation and providing positive ways forward. It would be easy, given the pace and sometimes questionable nature of change — what Barnett (2008) refers to as supercomplexity — to provide a simple critique of all that is wrong with the current situation and the foreseeable future. We are concerned, though, that to focus mainly on what is wrong or limiting in present circumstances, even where realistic, adds to the feelings of powerlessness and disconnect which some practitioners in education already experience. Our work, and the focus of the book, is exploring how individuals and organisations can work in ways that recognise the fast pace of change where supporting effective professional development enhances all aspects of teaching and learning. This means moving away from simple or quick-fix notions of professional development to ones that are critical, pragmatic, informed and flexible. Although much is written about professional development, and we draw upon these works throughout, it is often focused on the organisation, the individual or a response to policy. What is missing for us is a way of looking at the complex and changing interrelationships as a whole, seeing where change in one area affects other areas producing both intended and unintended consequences. To explore this relationship we have developed a model for critical professional development linking the individual, the organisation and the wider context, showing possibilities for individuals and for organisations. Turning our ideas into a model provides a mechanism to support discussion and understanding of areas of challenge and developing areas of opportunity. In a time of global recession and national austerity it is particularly significant to understand the wider context, incorporating policy and national bodies, interpreting the implications at both organisational and personal professional levels. To do so provides the understanding, if not always the direct opportunity, to plan and to develop professionally.

Rather than seeing the wider context, the organisation and the individual as separate entities within professional identity and development, we are interested in exploring how they relate to each other. At what points, and in what ways, is each potentially in conflict, mutually reinforcing or in a state of dissonance with each other? We discuss the way that looking at this interrelationship within a complex and bigger picture illustrates the forces that shape some of our professional experiences. More importantly, this wider view shows the spaces and structures that can be ~~ within and across the interrelationships for self-action ~~ment, by both individuals and organisations. The book, ~~ a simple 'how to' guide to achieving critical profes- ent. It is rather an exploration of the interrelationships, ions, motivations and rewards of undertaking develop-

2

ment as a professional educator. To do this we introduce the concept of professional capital to explore the individual and organisational value of critical professional development. We explain this concept in relation to our model, providing case studies as practical examples illustrating how professional capital can be both an individual and organisational invest-ment. Also key, and outlined in the case studies, are space and structure; these we term enabling structures and learning spaces. At an individual level the model and concepts can identify where, supported through critical self-reflection and collaboration, individual action and agency can be developed. We use several case studies to illustrate how the con-cept of professional capital can help to understand the individual and organisational benefit of investing in professional development.

Using the book

The book is organised into three parts. Part One looks at how current discussion and debate shape both public and private meaning of being a professional. As this is a key term we look at how its meaning has, and continues to be, contested, developed and rearticulated within education discourse. We discuss the importance of self-reflection within many models of professional formation or professional development, stressing the need for reflection to be critical and active. We locate our discussion within the fields of further and higher education, noting the role of policy and professional bodies as key drivers in current professional standards and qualifications. Following on from this we introduce and explain our concept of professional capital, drawing upon the work of Bourdieu (1989, 1998) showing how this concept enables us to link individual professionalism and organisational factors. In this first section we introduce our model of critical professional development. Developing our ideas into a model shows the interrelationship between the wider context, the organisation and the individual where professional development is enabled and enacted through policy, organisations or practitioner-led activity. We argue for the centrality of learning within this; learning that is socially and culturally constructed as well as being situated and contextual. From our experience we observe that learning doesn't just happen, it needs – amongst other things – time and support. Here we introduce our concepts of learning spaces and enabling structures to show how individuals and organisations can develop spaces and structures to support critical professional development.

Part Two looks at examples in practice, discussing four case studies which cover a range of professional practice. In this section we are joined by colleagues Lynne Barnes and Christine Hough who add different experiences to our own. The case studies span further and higher education and together represent formal, informal, organisational, practitioner and project work. Each shows the spaces and structures that the authors have used, or created, to support professional development in their work as teachers, developers or researchers – often a combination of all three. Lynne Barnes describes her experience of working with non-traditional learners in constructing an award programme for training deaf people to teach. Ruth Pilkington explores the construction of a progression framework for formal continuing professional development for educators in further and higher education. Christine Hough illustrates her work in moving early years higher education students from simple knowledge acquisition to critical thinking. Lastly, Yvon Appleby describes how she used writing for professional development in differing settings; from further to higher education with both inexperienced and experienced writers.

Part Three considers meanings, applications and approaches, using our model to discuss how opportunities may be applied and developed by individuals and the organisations they work in. To do this we unpack the individual case studies, discussing in concrete terms where opportunities have been developed, or exploited, to enable the conditions for critical professional development. We look at how each, responding to different needs and challenges with different groups and individuals, uses spaces and structures to create the potential for critical professional development. Finally we draw together the discussion of our model, focusing on recommendations for practice for organisations.

The book can be used in different ways. Parts may be used individually to reflect critically on personal careers exploring structured professional development. The case studies may be used as teaching material to stimulate group dialogue around the interrelationships between individuals, organisations and the wider context. This may support critical exploration of where we are placed individually and where we may want to change our position to operate more effectively. The model itself may be used to stimulate discussion about where both potential and challenge exist in the complex interrelationship between the wider context, organisations and individuals. The concept of professional capital may enable dialogue and negotiation between individuals and organisations. It may help to argue the case for a less instrumental and more pragmatic approach to sustainable individual and organisational development. This may be through using concrete examples of the practical applications of our concepts of enabling structures and learning spaces. In discussing and supporting professional development in organisations one of the challenges for practitioners working to achieve change is to acquire or develop the language to communicate ideas and this book provides concrete suggestions on how to do this.

Developing the book

Writing this book represents for us a positive opportunity for our own individual and collective critical professional development; it is a real example of our learning model in action. Initial ideas were shared through discussion and reflective dialogue between the two authors based upon their shared practices in teaching, educational and course development. Developing a framework of critical learning opportunities for the professional educators we work with has meant that over time we have experimented with ideas and practices: some have been jettisoned on the way and others are part of what we write about here. In addition, producing this work as a book has required us to develop different ways of working and communicating, as here we use a textual medium. To do this we have challenged our assumptions and questioned some of our beliefs and practices. Both of us have brought something different, and both of us have learned from the other as we created something together.

This writing process was expanded, becoming a dialogic community as, at times, four of us worked together, talking, reflecting and writing the case studies. Although this has been an extra activity to fit into already very busy work schedules, we all agree that we have valued the space and structure that contributing to the book has given us. We have made the space and time to talk about aspects of our work that we don't always have the opportunity to. We have written individually and collectively to share our work with others, again something we don't always find the time to do. In addition, we have discovered shared aspects of our work, which may lead us to work together in the future, whilst recognising the unique contribution that each of us individually strives to make to our own and others' professional development.

Part One

Professional development

Introduction to Part One

In the first chapter we talk about the reasons behind our definition of critical professional development. We do this because, as we discuss, the term has various meanings and is central to our ideas and our work. We describe three different approaches to professional learning, highlighting the impact of reflection as we discuss the contribution of each to professional learning and development. In an examination of how professionalism has changed, we draw specifically upon further and higher education and the implementation of professional standards within both sectors. We then introduce and explore the concept of professional capital to explore how this might help education practitioners and organisations engage with the challenges of the new educational environment. Finally, we identify key components of critical professionalism, which we offer as a way of responding to these challenges.

In the second chapter we move on to explore the model for critical professional development which encapsulates and communicates our ideas and work. We explain the model in detail, as well as the significance of enabling structures and learning spaces as fundamental components within it. To do this we discuss the value of basing the model on learning and then unpack learning spaces and enabling structures, further focusing on two aspects: communities of practice and the value of dialogue. The two chapters in this first part lay out the principles and theory informing the central argument of the book: that critical professional development cannot be seen simply as a linear individual or organisational response to external change; it requires a flexible, pragmatic approach based upon communication and recognition of the complexity of the sector and the contexts we work in.

CHAPTER ONE

The context for professional development

Introduction

Before it is possible to talk about professional development we need to consider what we mean by professionalism, as this is a term in education which is much used, and some would argue misused or abused. We draw upon the work of others here to illustrate our understanding and position. What does being a professional mean? Is it a quality you learn, acquire or are recognised as having? Is it something earned or bestowed? Is it always developing, and do we ever get there? Looking at the term historically suggests that rather than possessing a simple definition it can be viewed as an artificial construct that evolves and has changed over time (Crook, 2008). Traditional differences between and within professions have given way to more flexible and fluid meanings (Fenwick, 2009). Simple distinctions have clearly changed and with them our understanding of what it means to be professional and how it is defined (Evans, 2008). Jocelyn Robson (2006) argues, and we would agree, that 'profession' is a socially constructed and contested term that has different meanings attached to it by different people at different times. Robson provides a useful historical background, showing the wide range of meanings used by different approaches in the study of professions.

Part of what we understand as critical professional development is to recognise that we need to actively explore how we as individuals define ourselves and how we are externally defined as professionals in further and higher education. Being a professional can provide an individual and collective identity with agreed values, recognised responsibilities and acceptable or required behaviour in a particular field of practice.

Within a professional community an individual constructs a personal identity which provides a sense of belonging to others with shared or similar beliefs or values. Professionalism may be collectively established and maintained by a professional body through membership, codes of conduct, standards and review. To belong, an individual must qualify and be externally accepted for membership within what might be a closed or regulated group. Once external validation is achieved, however, there may be little support or motivation to continue to develop professionally. This presents something of a conundrum, particularly in education. Standards, codes of conduct and review may both frame what it means to be a professional and also prevent some educators from being supported, or seeing the need, to continue their professional development. We would argue that there is a need to continually develop ourselves professionally, particularly as the field of education is complex and fast-changing in response to economic, social and global issues. We therefore need to be able to analyse and respond to this dynamic situation which frames our identity and everyday practice. If we do not, we risk being overwhelmed by external change.

This chapter considers what is meant by being professional, exploring how the term of professionalism has developed, changed and become embedded in mainstream educational language and discourse. We discuss ways in which professionalism has been explained and articulated in several models and approaches, enabling us to construct our understanding and to explore its significance. In the first section we discuss various models that have supported understanding of professionalism within education. Then we go on to discuss how the critical professional is 'different from', and 'more than', as suggested in various reflective models of professional development. We emphasise the need to develop criticality and a critical consciousness in any reflective process. In the third section we consider how professionalism has been constructed, and more recently deconstructed, in further and higher education through the implementation of standards and the use of qualification awards and the licence to practice. In the fourth section we discuss how individual and organisational meanings of professionalism, often in conflict, may be understood within the concept of professional capital. In the closing section we introduce our definition of critical professionalism and signal the importance of learning, which for us is an essential component of critical professional development. This is the basis for our understanding and the model we offer for exploring and supporting critical professionalism.

12

Theoretical approaches to professionalism

The terms used to talk about professionalism, sometimes also referred to as professionality, can be seen to be constructed, contested and changed over time (Evans, 2008). Although writers have conceptualised professionalism in a variety of ways, at its core it is understood as professional knowledge informing professional practice. Three groups of theories emerge as significant:

- the knowledge model
- the career path model
- the 'doing and becoming' model.

The knowledge model

Of the three, perhaps the most concrete starting point is the 'knowledge model'. Aristotle introduced the notion of technical knowledge versus professional knowledge, where technical knowledge can be seen as a set of skills, competences or tools that a skilled technician applies within an educational setting. This is an approach that has been widely applied in further education. Professional knowledge implies a very different relationship where the emphasis is on beliefs, attitudes and values informing the work of a scholarly, 'wise' practitioner. Here, rather than simply being a technician, the professional makes and implements decisions on the basis of understanding, power and agency. Although much of what professionals in education do is mired in the humdrum, the routine, and systems and processes, at the same time the setting is hugely complex, dynamic and intensely challenging. This requires a capacity that is founded upon professional understandings and knowledge and which goes beyond simple technical competence. It is akin to the Aristotelian concept of *phronesis*, which we explore later.

The forms of knowledge associated with teaching are variously defined. Shulman is helpful for his identification of different types of knowledge that are core to professional functioning, embracing pedagogy, roles, responsibilities, the subject perspective and context (Shulman, 1987). His knowledge list, below, has retained its relevance and remains valuable with respect to current discussion of professional knowledge within policy and professional bodies. The list includes:

- content knowledge
- general pedagogic knowledge
- curriculum knowledge
- pedagogical content knowledge
- learners and their characteristics
- educational contexts
- knowledge of educational purposes.

The significance of professional knowledge is also central in Barnett's model of curriculum design – showing how professionals use their knowledge to support teaching and learning activity (Barnett, Parry and Coate, 2001). Their model suggests interlocking components which are essential in any curriculum, identifying three components fundamental to wider professional knowledge: action, knowledge and self. Knowledge here is the body of knowledge which is understood and applied in the field of education. This knowledge informs self, which in the model is about 'being' and includes identity and values. Action, underpinned by knowledge, is about the 'doing' of education, including behaviours and skills that are fundamental to a professional educator.

In her discussion of reflection, Kreber (2004) suggests that professionals can reflect on content, process and/or curricular knowledge. This discrimination between different types of knowledge ties in to Barnett's model above. In a less structured representation of knowledge, Fichtman and Yendol Hoppey (2008) talk about knowledge *for* practice, knowledge *in* practice and knowledge *of* practice. This accommodates development and the maturing of professionals. They identify different sources of each type of knowledge and different means of acquiring it. Knowledge for practice suggests engagement with a discrete body of knowledge that may be accessed through courses for beginning professionals; knowledge in practice suggests the doing of practice where tacit knowing emerges as professionals gain experience and expertise.

Another useful way of exploring professional knowledge is proposed by the 'Modes of Knowledge' model formulated by Gibbons *et al.* (1994) and developed by others (Scott *et al.*, 2004). It is a powerful analytical tool for exploring the different knowledge and knowledge environments that professionals occupy, or are located within. Gibbons (1994) described two modes of knowledge to account for the different types of knowledge that practitioners developed in their professional practice. Mode 1 is characterised as disciplinary knowledge, where the assumption is that this knowledge is superior to knowledge produced in the workplace. Mode 2 is characterised as technical rationality, where knowledge is socially accountable, has clear objectives and is located in and applied to practice.

The concept of modes of knowledge has been developed and extended in the work of Scott *et al.* (2004), who add two additional modes. Mode 3 is characterised by applied, practice-based knowledge taught to students using particular pedagogic means. Individual development occurs through reflection where knowledge is context specific and contextualised. Mode 4, characterised as critical knowledge, is political, change-oriented and often impact-oriented. This mode of knowledge is more action-oriented as it seeks to problematise, understand, influence or change external structures. The modes of knowledge model is useful in exploring the types of knowledge professionals work with, often navigating between several changing meanings as they develop in their career. For us, modes 3 and 4 are important as they acknowledge the process of knowledge development for practitioners which is centred on experiential learning.

The career path model

The career path model builds on the knowledge model as it focuses on tracking and responding to the career and professional life-cycle of the individual. It is a helpful construct because it asks questions targeting stage and need at specific career points. These models acknowledge that as careers change and develop so do professional identity and professional learning needs. They use ideas from Eraut (2000: 219) with a shift from competence towards expert knowledge. The suggestion is of a professional life-cycle that passes from early career to a middle phase and then to a period of maturity or, as Fuller terms it, 'professionalism' (1970, in Eraut, 1994: 72).

A career model can accommodate tensions experienced by many teachers in further and, increasingly, higher education who have established vocational expertise and who need to acquire expertise as teachers rapidly. New teachers may find confidence in their subject knowledge challenged by their novice career status as a teacher (Peel, 2005; Pill, 2005; Bathmaker and Avis, 2007). The career model shows how the middle phase of individual professional development centres on practice in the field and in the practice setting. This occurs through acquisition of new roles and responsibilities supported by reflective and

15

experiential learning (Boud, Keogh and Walker, 1985) and acquisition of artistry (Eisner, 1985). The period of mature practice can be characterised by frustration, dissatisfaction and disengagement, or by leadership and renewal, depending upon the individual and organisational context.

The career structure of education traditionally means that career progress in the classroom teacher role is limited. In many branches of education, promotion and career progression may require a gradual loss of focus on teaching that motivates the individual and characterises professional values. Career progress in further and higher education may mean entering managerial roles disassociated from actual teaching practice. In higher education in particular, career progress has been linked to an increased focus on research activity driven by research assessment exercises and performance.

The 'doing and becoming' model

The 'doing and becoming' model in professional development focuses on identity creation. The model proposes that when individuals learn they are individually constructing their own identity as part of discursive processes in a context and with the communities to which they belong. This model provides us with the notion of the individual as a cultural construct (Robson, 2006: 66) who learns through a process of deconstructing and reconstructing professional understanding and knowledge. This occurs through interaction with others and with the environment and is interpreted through background and prior assumptions and learning (Haigh, 2005; Vloet, Jacobs and Veugelers, 2013).

The idea of learning professionals, which Robson articulates as thinking and doing, is explored by other writers, for example Guile and Lucas (1999). They also see the significance of active learning for the learning professional described as someone who:

> *seeks out opportunities within whatever institutional constraints are in place, to extend their professional understandings and skills sets rather than being concerned merely to reflect on those they already possess.* (Guile and Lucas, 1999:163)

The idea of continual and active learning is widely shared: Grossman, Hammermas and McDonald (2009) describe how professional knowledge and identity are woven around teaching; the professional is therefore created through the doing of teaching. For us, this is integral and part of the process of becoming a professional educator and, importantly, one who is critical.

Thinking and activity, or doing and becoming, are not enough in themselves — criticality is necessary. Workplace learning is helpful in exploring how individuals learn in different contexts and over time. Stephen Billett (2002), for example, conveys an idea of the practitioner 'always becoming' (in Robson, 2006: 73) discussing the mutual and reciprocal relationship between the workplace and individual. These writers point out that identity for the professional is complex in its formation and will change throughout the life of the individual and his/her workplace context.

Reflection and reflective models of professionalism

Reflection has long been considered crucial to being a teacher or educational professional, becoming a fundamental component in professional learning and education processes. The ongoing development of professionals is often associated with the concept of reflective practice, but how does that relate to the notion of critical professionalism? Many of the factors we have found most useful have their roots in the work of early writers on the subject of reflection. For example Dewey (1938) talked of sense-making in reflection as a counter-measure for the individual teacher responding to issues that are problematic and generate perplexity or doubt. He placed considerable emphasis on the role of attitudes and emotion in reflective processes, the affective side of reflection. The issues of sense-making are important for us as they align strongly with how we conceptualise the professional as an individual learning within communities and local settings. For us Habermas (1974) offered useful insight as he discussed knowledge generation through reflection. Within his work he outlined aspects of self-knowledge, emancipation and empowerment leading to transformative outcomes for the practitioner. This is particularly relevant within the complex professional settings where we work. In addition, Van Manen's (1991) proposal for levels of reflection are helpful: in particular, his ideas of reflecting on processes of reflection, which is identified as meta-reflection. In our work and our thinking meta-reflection is essential, as it encourages the professional practitioner to step back beyond simply reflecting on immediate issues and problems. A more analytical form of reflection is necessary for effective professional development because it allows the individual to engage with the messy landscape of practice and the individual's place within it. It enables new perspectives on individual identity, workplace context, professional role and the influences upon the individual to emerge.

Whilst Kolb (1984) and Schon (1983) arguably have led the field in articulating ideas of learning from, and reflecting on, experience, it is Boud (in Boud, Keogh and Walker, 1985) whose work contributes much to the value of reflection as socially constructed. Much of what Boud *et al.* (1985, cited in Moon 1999: 30) say about reflection informs our views of social constructivism as an underpinning model of learning: that learning is socially constructed and socially experienced. For us, therefore, learning is historical, contextual and contingent.

Boud *et al.* discuss how the professional learns through reflection through the following four stages:

- by association of new data to existing knowledge;
- by seeing relationships and integration;
- by a process of cross-checking – checking the validity of new information or checking assumptions and preconceptions;
- finally, by appropriation – making the knowledge one's own.

A key component of critical concepts of reflection is that professionals are encouraged to move beyond self-referential approaches (Brookfield, 1995) and to engage purposefully with wider views, including policy, others' perspectives and theory. Tools such as logs, critical incidents, peer review, action research and mentoring can all support this. What is implied but not always made explicit is a dialogic approach to reflection. This emphasises participation within communities of practice to generate shared codified and communicable meanings. In this, the role of the 'peer', the 'facilitator', the 'mentor' and the 'critical friend' makes a huge contribution to reflection and the learning of the individual teacher (Trevitt and Perera, 2009). Overall, the shift towards a more critical approach to reflection fits with Larrivee's (2008: 353) tool to assess levels of reflection. We find Larrivee's approach useful as it emphasises the wider perspectives, values and understanding of external influence.

We assert that critical reflection can be applied variously across a range of roles, activities and professional practice:

1. The generic body of professional knowledge associated with courses and education for professionals at the beginning of their

careers. This helps the novice teacher begin to make links between the discrete knowledge base of the field and their practice, creating a foundation for their own knowledge construction.

2. The acquisition of professional 'artistry', which may be more context specific and which is developed through reflection on and around practice and is suitable for growing or maturing professionals.

3. The development of professionals as leaders and constructors of the professional knowledge base within communities of practice. In this case, reflection involves interrogating assumptions and meta-reflection so that the individual can contribute to changes and the development of the communal knowledge base.

4. The emergence of the practitioner-researcher as a professional construct. Here the practitioner systematically explores practice to develop new professional knowledge and engages with its construction 'reflexively'.

Becoming a professional is not a one-off or static activity. Supporting professional career trajectories requires a range of tools suitable for different contexts across a changing professional life-span. These tools may encourage professionals to engage with their own 'taken-for-granted' assumptions and beliefs, their cultural and educational constructs (Ghaye and Ghaye, 1998). This process needs to incorporate reflection on underlying power structures, questioning established beliefs that are being played out within their practice domain. For us, critical reflection and the associated reflective tools are applied and situated around action, praxis and professional judgement and empowerment. Reflection, then, is one part of theorising on becoming and developing as a professional. What it means to be a professional in education is, as we suggest, not static; it is mediated, influenced and shaped by individual understandings and values as well as external constraints and expectations. For this reason, reflection that is critical is essential.

Further and higher education: Constructing and deconstructing professionalism

As we write, the field of post-compulsory education is fast-changing and dynamic as both further education and higher education sectors respond to recent policy directives and policy recommendations. For example, in higher education, changes in tuition fees, deregulation of degree-awarding powers and a reduction of the widening participation agenda (Doyle and Griffin, 2012) has had an impact upon the number and background of students. In further education, the emphasis has been on teachers, with recommendations to change the initial teacher training programmes and qualifications of those who teach in this sector (Department for Business, Innovation and Skills, 2012d). These changes are altering the identity and practice of professionals in both sectors: some changes may be viewed as positive, others less so. Whilst change is an important aspect of creating a vital and responsive education system, many question the top-down nature of some of the changes and the consequences, both intended and unintended, for those who work in both sectors.

In contrast to school teaching, which is nationally regulated, teaching in further and higher education is historically less tightly controlled, as many teachers entered as professionals with specific disciplinary or vocational knowledge. In further education, this may be as a professional chef who teaches cooking, or a veterinary nurse with professional qualifications who teaches a Foundation Degree. Often, awarding bodies, for example City and Guilds in further education or an internal quality assurance unit in higher education, require teaching staff to hold appropriate professional qualifications. It has increasingly been the focus of criticism and debate in both sectors that not enough emphasis is placed on teachers being developed and recognised as teaching professionals as well as subject specialists. In further education, reviews such as Foster (2005) prompted the move to professionalise a workforce hitherto unregulated and un-professionalised. Angela Stewart (2009: 13) comments that the lack of required teaching qualifications in further education pre-2001 will indeed come to seem incredible.

The move towards professionalising the further education sector is covered in detail elsewhere (for example, see Hillier, 2006; Robson, 2006; Stewart, 2009), but a brief summary is useful to show how this sector has been professionalised, and is being potentially de-professionalised, in a short space of time. Prior to 2001, although some individuals were qualified, there was no requirement for teachers in the further education sector to be qualified. In 2001, regulations for qualifications were introduced but were limited to teachers in colleges. However, an Ofsted survey on initial teacher training of further education teachers reported that the system in place was not satisfactory (Ofsted, 2003) and called for changes to be made. The significance of 'expert' teachers was outlined in the 2006 White Paper *Further Education: Raising Skills, Improving Life Chances* based around six key areas for improvement (for summary, see Hillier, 2006; 111), setting out a vision for learner achievement supported by expert subject teaching by qualified, skilled teachers. This resulted in a suite of new qualifications for further education being introduced in 2007; qualifications that developed the standards set out by the Further Education National Training Organisation (FENTO), the previous regulating body. The new qualifications were underpinned by standards from Lifelong Learning UK (LLUK), a Sector Skills Council, with continuing professional development, a requirement to qualify and maintain a licence to practice, managed by the Institute for Learning (IfL). The take-up of the qualifications has been reported as resulting in 80 per cent of all teaching staff in further education colleges having, or working towards, recognised teaching qualifications, with 57 per cent above Level 5 (Department for Business, Innovation and Skills, 2012a). Thus, in a comparatively short space of time, between 2001 and 2012, the further education sector can be said to have been professionalised, as individuals have been required to become qualified teachers continuing their professional development to achieve and maintain a licence to practice.

However, the Lingfield Interim Report on professionalism published in March 2012 (Department for Business, Innovation and Skills, 2012b) made recommendations which suggested overturning qualification requirements for teaching in the lifelong learning sector. This produced a vigorous response from the sector, including the unions and professional bodies, expressing concern about de-professionalising the workforce. The government response (Department for Business, Innovation and Skills, 2012c) conceded that deregulation of teaching registration and professional development was impossible within the proposed timescale, but as existing requirements were unworkable it was a reprieve rather than a full-scale change. The final Lingfield Report, delivered in October 2012 (Department for Business, Innovation and Skills, 2012d: 22), further supported this change by defining professionalism for this sector and how it might flourish 'without interference'. The description is therefore significant. Professionalism is defined as:

- mastery of a complex discipline;
- continuous enhancement of expertise;

- acceptance that the field of expertise is a vocation to be pursued selflessly for the benefit of others;
- public accountability for high standards of capability and conduct;
- membership of a group earning and deserving the respect of the community;
- membership of a defined group with similar skills, transcending local loyalties to achieve national and international recognition;
- acceptance of responsibility for the competence and good conduct of other members of the professional group;
- membership of a group which accepts responsibility for planning succession by future generations;
- membership of a group which seeks continuously to extend and improve its field of knowledge;
- membership of a group deserving an above-average standard of living.

Rather than being regulated through externally imposed standards and bodies, this new arrangement is proposed to be managed in the context of a new covenant or compact relationship between employers and staff and a guild to act as a professional body for the further education sector. This change in policy has produced many paradoxes: the further education sector is being challenged to deliver skills for sustainable growth (Department for Business, Innovation and Skills, 2010) and staff professionalism is seen as vital to achieving this (Department for Business, Innovation and Skills, 2011) in spite of being deregulated. This is discussed more fully in a special edition of *Adults Learning* (2012) and in Hillier and Appleby (2012), where we argue that, whilst some changes may have been necessary, these changes represent a see-saw approach to policy. This deregulation overturns previous moves to professionalise the further education sector, where all teachers were to be qualified, reverting to one that relies on individualised professionalism.

In the higher education sector, the impulse, prompted by increased accountability and quality assurance, has been to raise the profile of teaching as part of the academic's role and responsibilities, alongside research, income-generation and administration. This has been formally achieved through a series of consultations and initiatives throughout the 1990s, enhancing teaching quality and developing a body of pedagogic understanding specifically aimed at higher education. The process has been complemented by the gradual introduction and establishment of a professional framework of standards for teaching and learning, the UK Professional Standards Framework (UKPSF). Creating a professional body in higher education began with the launch of the Institute of Learning and Teaching (ILT) which built on the Teacher Accreditation Scheme introduced by the Staff and Educational Development Association (SEDA) in 1993. The early ILT focused on individual membership through application and submission of evidence. There were continuing professional development responsibilities but these were poorly defined. This was replaced by the UK Professional Standards Framework (PSF) in 2006. As a professional framework it was subtly different to that of the ILT in that institutions, rather than individuals, are the members and so it is institutions that assume responsibility and ultimately authority for the professional development and recognition of staff within the framework. This alters the relationship between the individual and the professional body and potentially strengthens the emphasis on accountability and performance of the individual with respect to the employing organisation.

The UK PSF applies criteria of academic responsibility and knowledge, relating primarily to the concept of a lecturer/researcher within the Bologna sense of the term (Magna Charta Universitatum, 18 September 1988: 2). Re-launched in 2011 it embraces, to some extent, higher education professionals working in different roles: in student support, postgraduate research students, ad hoc lecturers, a research lead, or a manager within higher education. The framework adopts a vision of professionals progressively engaging within academic work to enhance the student experience, shifting from peripheral participation to leadership at local and national levels.

UK PSF identifies core knowledge for the professional educator which is both about the subject and the way to teach and support learning of the subject. In this it reflects Shulman's professional knowledge list discussed earlier. The core values additionally set out the professional moral base and ethic of the professional educator. What is more, the UK PSF contains an expectation in the values section of the documentation that the professional educator should be motivated to pursue improvement and enhancement of the learning experience in order to better serve the students. The suggestion is this should be informed by scholarship, research, professional development and evidence-based practice.

The UK Professional Standards Framework (2011) is encouraging institutions to focus on developing practice in higher education in line with the professional ethos of an academic who is a scholar of both the discipline and teaching and learning (Healey, 2001: Brew, 2010). The new framework contains two specific statements that reinforce the value of a progressive, formal construction for developing the higher education academic focusing on the primacy of research. The first specifically identifies a dimension within the range of activities considered core to the academic role. This is accompanied by a value statement to support evidence-informed approaches and the outcomes from research, scholarship and continuing professional development. Together these act to emphasise the central role played by research and scholarship with respect to teaching and learning practices as part of the professional profile of the higher education academic.

Professional capital: Linking individuals and organisational meanings

The picture that emerges across both sectors is that the type of professional knowledge which has frequently been recognised and valued has largely been technicist in tone. It can be argued that the move towards marketisation, managerialism and a performance-related culture does little to disrupt the pervasive nature of this approach. Across higher education this tendency occurs within a specialist knowledge base where academics are constructors and disseminators of knowledge. Here, the idea of professionalism has tended to prioritise the specialist nature of the knowledge field and ownership of that knowledge (see for example discussion of mobilisation of knowledge in Fenwick and Farrell, 2012). Further educators have frequently been characterised as operating within an applied knowledge context in which knowledge creation and ownership is often seen from a master–apprentice perspective, potentially reducing innovation (Bathmaker and Avis, 2005).

For both sectors more recently there has been a shift in what is traditionally understood by professional knowledge, how it can be acquired and the value placed upon it. Professional knowledge, therefore, is in a state of flux, moving from something discrete to a more fluid notion of contingent professional knowledge. In this way professional knowledge is associated with the individual in a workforce where competition and market forces predominate. What is more, the changes are ongoing and accelerating. The result is increasing competition between institutions, with individual as well as organisational accountability driven by targets, measurement and quantifiable determinants. Underpinning these trends are significant changes to governance and the use of research and organisational data as a new governing mode to ensure individual and organisational performance and accountability (Ozga, 2012).

This changing landscape has led to the emergence of the radically different concept of what it is to be a professional, described by Stephen Ball in 2003, where teachers are reframed as producers. Later, Ball (2008) argued that professionals are being shaped by performance activity, privatisation and governance. The emergence of a performance-related culture, over several governments, has increased compliance through the regulation and definition of teaching and learning performance. The emphasis on individual performance may create new opportunities for some but, as Avis argues, it attacks the professional autonomy of the many (Avis, 2010).

At an organisational level this can be seen in the regulation of awards, in quality assurance and in continuing professional development increasingly being linked to appraisal and individual targets. These examples are explained in Ball's (2008) analysis of the technologies of educational reforms which he locates within Foucault's notion of the power of discourse supporting regulatory regimes. At an individual level, Ball points out, these educational reforms increase stress, increase the intensification and pace of work with more paperwork, and result in greater surveillance of work and outputs (2008: 52). These may be at variance with personal beliefs or understanding of professionalism. Much recent reform in education is about growth and development, increasingly being framed within the notion of a product or commodity; one which has economic capital and value. Drawing upon Bourdieu's work we have found the notion of 'professional capital' useful to understand personal and institutional investment, transaction and value in terms of teacher professionalism.

Capital is a useful concept as it can be both real and symbolic, signifying the value of social, cultural and economic relations of power. Bourdieu's work has been used in this way to explore professionalism in related fields such as nursing (Moreberg, Lagerstrom and Dellve, 2011) and for community action to alleviate social injustice (Kang and Glassman, 2010). Discussing social capital in relation to education, John Field (2008) noted that this concept had brought an awareness and interest in the 'payoff' that arises from our social–professional relationship. This is useful, as from our perspective it can be argued that such 'payoff' can have both positive and negative consequences professionally. This allows us to explore some of the tensions between the individual, the organisation and the wider context where, as individuals, we are being externally shaped as well as individually constructing and developing our professional capital. By professional capital we mean the knowledge, practices, social relations and experience of being a teacher. This is located within a system which places value, increasingly an economic value, on those skills and knowledge, valuing it as capital increasingly not for investment but for profit. Bourdieu (1998) argues that neoliberal discourse, a pervasive force behind most social and economic power relations, does not recognise collectives but increasingly focuses on individuals. In education, as in other fields, he comments that this can be interpreted as an absolute reign of flexibility which is experienced by professionals through short-term contracts, individual objectives, individual appraisal and financial reward based upon individual competence and merit (1998: 97). Whilst the prevailing discourse in education may be of choice, autonomy and the increased value of professionalisation, the reality for many may be in stark contrast.

The gap between discourse and lived experience is discussed by Stephen Ball (2006; 49), drawing upon Foucault's notion of regimes of truth. He identifies significant differences between what are represented as professional values for recruitment and those which can be categorised as being recognised as having market value. Professional values for teachers, he argues, are codified as: responding to individual needs; supporting commonality and open access; serving community needs; allocating resources to those in most need; valuing collectivism; and having a broad assessment of professional worth. In contrast, he observes the market values and rewards: individual teacher performance; teachers using streaming and exclusion; using resources for the most able; competition; and individual narrow assessment of performativity.

The notion of professional capital enables the professionalism of teachers to be seen as a dual concept; both as something individually developed (personal value) and at the same time as something which is externally constructed and regulated (use value). Teaching is a professional role and identity which has simultaneous intrinsic and extrinsic value as well as individual, social and cultural meaning. Understanding how teachers navigate their individual personal beliefs within a socially constructed and regulated meaning of their professional identity gives a different perspective to the idea of dual professionalism.

It also helps to explain some of the tension in managing two or more potentially competing value bases.

In the current climate, which privileges marketisation and managerialism, educational organisations may focus on the economic rationale of capital which views knowledge, competence, skills and experience as economic currency and capital value. The skills, knowledge and experience which make up professional capital can thus be mobilised in the service of the organisation to achieve strategic objectives and targets motivated by market and economic drivers. In contrast, individual professional capital may reflect ideas of one's knowledge, artistry, experience, values and beliefs. This may include career decisions informed by values which are based upon the principle of service and a commitment to education.

Part of the development of professional capital, which may be both explicitly and implicitly acquired, is an understanding of how things are done at an organisational and systems level. The difficult position teachers find themselves in is where the institutional understanding of capital is dominant and overrides the individual's own sense of professional capital. Such a professional dissonance echoes Bourdieu's argument that the work contract adopted within the neoliberal discourse fosters a sense of unworthiness with a constant need for individuals to prove themselves (Bourdieu, 1998, 1999). Stephen Ball describes this as alienation of self, where:

> *Teachers are no longer encouraged to have a rationale for practice, an account of themselves in terms of a relationship to the meaningfulness of what they do, but are required to produce measurable and improving outputs and performances; what is important is* what works. (Ball, 2006: 150; original emphasis)

Operating in the environment of commodification and marketisation, within which, arguably, most educational organisations now function, the individual can feel disempowered if she/he continues to operate according to former, now increasingly obsolete, parameters of professionalism and identity. The lack of fit between competing external and internal notions of professionalism can be experienced as a growing sense of frustration, cynicism and stress in which individual understanding does not engage with the ways that the wider drivers are affecting current practice and shaping professional identity.

Understanding that professional capital can be interpreted differently by an organisation and an individual enables exploration of potentially competing agendas. This requires a renegotiation of the professional contract around the question of professional capital. To do this, the organisation has to engage with what professional capital might mean in a more expansive way: one that is not bounded by a simple economic value of capital. Rather, an organisation needs to invest in the skills, knowledge and expertise developed by the professionals themselves through professional learning and continuing professional development. An awareness of how this is being enacted by both organisation and individual allows each to reframe tools for agency, and to restructure processes that build capacity and capability. This can be integrated within a proactive dual-loop, or even triple-loop, perspective as suggested in the work of Argyris and Schon (1995). Here, development is seen as a reinforcing and reinforming cycle.

Blockages and fracture emerge where organisations insist on assuming a managerialist approach in which the dialogue, reframing and collaborative restructuring of the professional contract is ignored or is imposed. This cannot be a long-term default position, as at some point, Bourdieu reminds us (1998: 102), if capital is not renewed it will eventually run out. If institutions are unwilling, or unable, to invest in the development of the professional capital of their teachers, the teachers need to do it themselves, collectively (Sachs, 2001). The issue of collaborative reframing of the professional contract is increasingly significant within education, as the product of learning relies upon the individual practitioner and the relationships between learner and teacher, where individual levels of commitment, enthusiasm and inspiration play an important role in influencing the learning of students. It cannot simply be seen, or experienced, as a managed outcome.

The benefits to the individual of exploring their professional identities and practices through the notion of professional capital include:

1. **An increased sense of agency.** This is achieved through re-framing individual professional identity by taking account of 'me plc'. This requires that we individually review our skills and professional capital by taking ownership of our continuing professional development. In this way we develop, or maintain, a sense of professional worth rather than a more reductionist institutional use value.

28

2. **Employability.** By appreciating that most education sectors are dynamic and fast-changing we can develop a sense of our own professional worth in terms of employability by investing in our individual professional capital. This means making continuing professional development count, being aware of – or creating – opportunities to acquire new knowledge or skills which enhance and extend our employment opportunities.

3. **Collaboration and networking.** In understanding that many current educational practices support an individual banking model of capital, we can challenge this, using Freire's work (1972), by investing in shared professional networks, spaces and communities to exchange, share and develop collective critical knowledge.

4. **Refreshment and motivation.** Active engagement with our own professional capital development can counter frustrations and support the reflective processes that keep teaching 'fresh' (Bleakley *et al.*, 2003, cited in Robson, 2006: 88).

On an individual level there are disadvantages to not exploring professional identity and professional practices and to accepting the status quo in terms of professional capital. These include:

1. **Increased cynicism.** As more is required within a market-driven education system, particularly in the higher and further education sectors, it is possible to feel devalued and cynical about any change. Without a critical perspective all change feels as though it is simply more individual input for less overall educational value.

2. **A sense of lack of control.** By not engaging critically with the bigger picture, where contrasting and potentially competing views of professional capital exist between the institution and the individual it is possible to feel a sense of alienation and lack of control about the educational experience being produced.

3. **A sense of imposed agenda-shaping practice.** This adds to a sense of lack of control where little transformation or resistance to external agenda, at policy or institutional level, is seen as possible.

There are real advantages for institutions engaging with the notion of professional capital that recognise the professional worth, not just the use value, and the benefit to the institutions of investing in their workforce.

These advantages include:

1. **A satisfied and engaged workforce.** By investing in individuals through continuing professional development, developing peer support systems and recognising existing skills, the workforce will be more satisfied and engaged. By investing in individuals rather than enforcing institutional compliance, workers may experience less stress, less illness and less disaffection and cynicism.
2. **Harmonisation of competing agendas.** By recognising that there are competing agendas, for example between policy, quality measures and educational processes, professional dialogue may be employed to produce effective and workable solutions which can be owned by both parties.
3. **Staff as co-creators and directors in their own continuing professional development.** This has advantages for the organisation, as continuing professional development can be targeted to most effectively develop existing skills and knowledge which will enhance the professional capital of the individual and the organisation.

There are disadvantages which may be experienced in the short term, although we would argue that these are outweighed by longer-term benefits. These include:

1. **Cost.** Some short-term costs may be incurred as disaffected staff move, are ill, or resist change in the process of revisiting the professional contract.
2. **A blame culture.** This may be created in the short term where the organisation has hitherto relied to a large extent on different tools, such as champions as individual agents leading change out of professional conviction. A process of institutional change may be experienced as unsettling.
3. **The changing influence of professional bodies as drivers for directing change.** Within what we signal as a time of significant change in education the landscape of professional bodies is shifting, creating new opportunities and new challenges. A good example of this in the further education sector is the creation of the Further Education Guild.

Using the notion of professional capital allows us to see how the shifting nature of professionalism has an impact on individuals as well as at institutional and sector level. At some points the intersections between them may be in harmony, but they may be in tension creating disunity and fracture. The notion of professional capital enables the organisation to recognise the value of professional development and investment in the individual. It also enables the individual to see the value of actively pursuing their own professional development, both as an independent professional educator and as a part of an educational organisation. Individual or organisational actions may be seen as potentially different but they can, using this concept, also be seen as mutually reinforcing.

Our understanding of critical professionalism

So far, we have discussed the context of professional development looking at the ways that meanings and practices surrounding this concept have been developed, reconfigured and changed. We have used the idea of professional capital to explore the shifting context of professionalism which is being continually shaped and reshaped by policy and through its implementation. We have looked at how professionalism has been constructed and deconstructed in further and higher education in recent decades, leading to potential fractures and imbalances between individual and organisational understanding, and investment in professional capital. In response we identify areas for individual practitioners that sustain and support the development of professional capital.

Our definition of critical professionalism

Our understanding of critical professionalism that supports our work and underpins the model which we discuss in the next chapter is outlined in six key characteristics. These characteristics enable individuals to:

1. Possess an appreciation of their individual professional capital and how to develop and apply it.
2. Identify and use selectively opportunities for learning purposefully to enhance self and practice becoming a learning professional.
3. Learn through critical reflection which is informed by values, wider understanding, scholarship, reflection on practice and interrogation of individuals' own assumptions and prior learning.
4. Become skilled in the multiple discourses that enable operation

31

across diverse communities for the purpose of sustaining and creating professional identity.

5. Develop awareness of the complex state and interplay of knowledge and practice.

6. Apply agency within the organisational context to make judgements and initiate actions on individuals' own and others' behalf with respect to practice, position and career.

These six characteristics are illustrated in Figure 1.1.

Figure 1.1 The component elements of critical professionalism

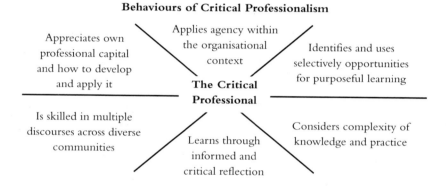

Behaviours of Critical Professionalism

Appreciates own professional capital and how to develop and apply it

Applies agency within the organisational context

Identifies and uses selectively opportunities for purposeful learning

The Critical Professional

Is skilled in multiple discourses across diverse communities

Learns through informed and critical reflection

Considers complexity of knowledge and practice

Precursors for Critical Professionalism

Whilst drawing upon existing work which emphasises knowledge creation, both from and for professional practice, we wish to foreground the importance of learning in professional development. To answer the questions that we started the chapter with, we do not believe that people simply earn professional status, or have it bestowed upon them. We do not believe that it is easy to acquire and even when externally recognised by others, we do not assume that it is fully formed or completed. We do believe, however, that it is always developing and we are in a process of always becoming through critical doing, thinking and being – in other words action, knowledge and self. In the next chapter we explore what we identify as learning spaces and enabling structures that support and shape some of these learning activities and processes.

CHAPTER TWO

Learning spaces and enabling structures for critical professional development

Introduction

In the previous chapter we discuss the different meanings and models which inform how being a professional in the field of education has been constructed and, we argue, is being deconstructed. It is a time of rapid change where what it means to be a professional is interpreted at an individual level as well as at organisational and policy levels. It is not enough in this supercomplex environment for the individual merely to reflect on his/her own teaching practice; nor is it enough for an organisation to treat its professionals as replaceable units to achieve measurable outcomes. In looking at the interrelationship between individuals and organisations we use the concept of professional capital to explore both agency and responsibility. As a critical professional, the individual practitioner needs to engage with her/his own values, assumptions and the influences of policy and organisational systems and processes. This critical perspective, based upon the responsibility to question the construction of professionalism more widely, can for its part support individual and collective agency. The organisation has a responsibility to support the development of professionals who have some degree of professional autonomy and agency. This benefits the institution by it becoming more fully a learning organisation (cf. Senge, 1990) supported by critical professionals able to contribute professional knowledge, insights and experience to teaching and learning.

We are aware that critical professional development doesn't just happen

– in fact much of what we hear in our own practice indicates that it is under attack. As education has increasingly become commodified (Ball, 2003), it can be argued that activities or actions which are viewed as process- rather than product-oriented are seen as professionally irrelevant by organisations. Aware of this, we have developed a model to show how individuals and organisations, both influenced by wider contexts, can be supported to explore and develop critical professionalism. In this chapter we build on ideas introduced at the end of Chapter One to focus on the enablers through which critical professionalism can be developed. It is not a simple template that can be applied to achieve a desired outcome; rather it provides a conceptual framing to see where possibilities may already occur, or where they can be developed both by individuals and/ or organisations. The model is based upon theories of learning which include structured, non-structured, informal and networked learning. Learning may be individual, collaborative, face-to-face or involve virtual learning experiences. We use the terms 'enabling structures' and 'learning spaces' to discuss how learning may be organised and structured to support critical professional development.

The chapter is divided into five sections, each addressing our model of critical professional development and the significance of enabling structures and learning spaces for this. We argue that key to this model, and much of the work upon which it is based, is understanding and sup-porting learning which is critical and reflexive and develops praxis. In the first section we explain our model, showing the interconnections, spaces and potential sites of fracture between individual and organisational activity and how it may have an impact on critical professional development. In the second section we show the significance of basing critical professional development on learning which is, we believe, socially constructed and situated. The third and fourth sections explore in more detail a range of enabling structures and learning spaces as ways of supporting critical professional development. We discuss how these are enacted at a variety of levels, unpacking our model for this chapter. Section five provides some concluding thoughts which show the link between the model we discuss and the case studies that follow.

A model of professional learning to support critical development

We have observed in our work with others, and in our own professional development, that when professionals learn they are individually constructing their own identity as part of a discursive process with and within the communities to which they belong (Barnett, 2008). The challenge we have identified is that this requires thinking space. Without time to reflect or analyse, any action may simply be a problem-solving response. In other words, learning becomes a single-loop process (Argyris and Schon, 1995). Given the pressures on individuals in the changing educational context to crisis manage and to balance numerous and increasing workloads and roles, this becomes a real threat to professional development. Rather than developing professional capital, this situation can be seen as exploiting the individual's professional resources. Through the introduction of learning spaces the individual can engage in thinking and reflective processes, allowing a critical perspective that enables responses for change from a position of understanding, self knowledge, and awareness of the consequences of action. In this way a more useful double-loop learning can be achieved, or even triple-loop (Argyris and Schon, 1995), through reflection and action based upon practical knowledge. In this way meta-reflection and meta-learning can occur and critical perspectives be acquired which lead to achievement of *phronesis*. For us, as for many others in education (for example, Plowright and Barr, 2012), the concept of *phronesis* is significant as it is based upon practical wisdom and ethical informed action. This is at the heart of our model, which shows how organisation and peer-initiated learning spaces can be purposefully utilised to support critical professional perspectives and learning. This is more than simple knowledge acquisition, and more than a 'one-off' training approach. It recognises and accommodates the way that education is structured and the changing nature of employing organisations, where change is often driven at meso- and macro-levels. The model shown in Figure 2.1 represents the levels and forms of the key enabling structures we have identified and employed within our own practice as teacher–educators.

In the model, the individual sits at the centre of three concentric circles representing tiers within which enabling structures and learning spaces can be enacted. The circles allow us to bring together the individual, the locations of learning and the ways in which a professional

Figure 2.1 A model for supporting critical professional development using enabling structures and learning spaces

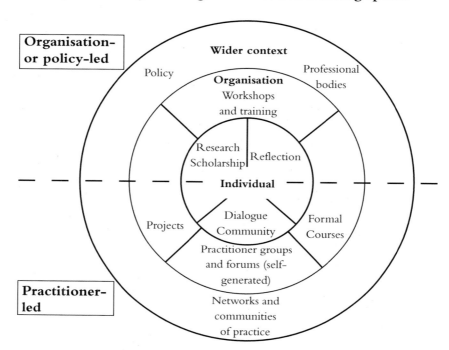

can learn. Placing the individual at the heart of the model is significant, as individual practitioners are the locus of professional knowledge, of professional insight and wisdom. The individual is more than just a small cog in a wheel; they are a person, who comes with a history, a unique place in the world and a sense of the future. The individual makes sense of the world for him/herself and, as a professional within the field of education, also helps others to makes sense of the world out there, past present or future, through a process of learning.

Whilst the individual is central, the model itself is divided into two halves to represent the way that individual learning can be practitioner-led or organisationally-led. The top half shows elements where organisations, or wider policy drivers, play a significant and primary role in shaping learning activity for the professional. In the lower half, shaping is largely instigated by the individual practitioners and is led by their interests and priorities. These two approaches are not, of course, mutually exclusive, as individual interest may be a result of policy changes; for example, practitioner groups working on Functional Skills, and organisations may support practitioner networks or research in responding to policy change and implementation in this area. The central circle identifies key elements through which the individual learns.

As a way of bridging and connecting the two halves we present a series of circles that reflect different tiers where learning spaces can be enacted and examined as well as the key structures for enabling learning within each tier. This provides a way of seeing existing and potential learning spaces and opportunities which will develop professional capital for both individuals and organisations. One of the difficulties we observe in our practice is that individuals sometimes find it hard to explain why their individual action may be beneficial to the organisation, or organisations struggle to explain the relevance of suitable updating and learning opportunities to individuals working across a range of subjects and age ranges. Two examples can illustrate this:

1. Joining a practitioner network might support a greater individual professional understanding which will in turn potentially enhance teaching and learning.
2. An organisation providing good-quality learning opportunities around safeguarding can generate outcomes that all practitioners find relevant.

At times it appears difficult to bridge the gap between the individual and the organisation in what is needed, wanted and valued professionally. Our model allows some of the interrelationships and linkages to be conceptualised and examined in terms of influences and impacts.

Circles of learning

Within the central circle in our model we focus on the individual practitioner. Here, learning takes place in practice largely through reflective learning, independent scholarship and discursive means. This is what Cunningham (2008) terms 'professional talk'. This is likely to be enacted through immediate practice and in the immediate setting or practice context. It may, therefore, involve dialogue with peers in a variety of naturally occurring situations, in the café or at the photocopier. As we have discussed, however, professional exchange of this type may remain situated within the individual's experience; to make it critical it also needs to be more widely informed (Eraut, 2004). This is where reflection, research or scholarship enables more rigorous and focused learning activity to take place. Alongside professional talk, individual practitioner learning is supported by scholarship and, ideally, research. Vloet, Jacobs and Veugelers (2013: 420) describe the goal for teachers as becoming 'adaptive, critical practitioner-researchers'. This aligns closely with our view and is what is frequently described in health professions as being evidence-based. If the individual's learning remains within this first, or inner, circle of influence and focus it may well be reflective but may potentially be too constrained by practice and local issues to become critical professionalism. It can, however, become critical professionalism for the individual, given structured space and enabling facilitation. Vloet, Jacobs and Veugelers (2013) emphasise that professional learning is achieved through dialogic activity, and Colley, James and Dinet (2007: 280) highlight space for learning and reflection. The first circle identifies all of these elements as crucial.

As this first circle sits within the centre of both halves of the model, it suggests that individual learning can also be motivated or instigated through organisational or role demands, or even through professional body requirements. This may be, for example, updating qualifications required by awarding bodies to retain a licence to practise. Motivation is important as it relates to agency, and hence it is important to acknowledge, too, the unspoken contribution of emotion and affective components (Beijaard, Meijer and Verloop, 2004; Evans, 2008) giving purpose, energy and agency to the central circle.

The second circle focuses on structures and systems that are constructed at an organisational level supporting the educational practitioner's learning around job roles and functions. This organisational level of learning may take the form of formal courses which focus on the learning of the professional; many postgraduate programmes in education are good examples of this. Within this second sphere of activity and responsibility, groups and forums may be established to respond to particular initiatives, tasks or issues (Wenger and Snyder, 2000). Projects, whether internally initiated or externally funded, make excellent organisational spaces, as they include specific resourcing around tasks and organisational goals. Examples of these include Learning and Skills Information Service (LSIS) practitioner research projects in further education and HE Academy practice-based projects. Finally, workshops and training provide structured space for professional development. However these are often limited by their capacity to transfer one-off learning into wider, long-term practice. This failing is often given as a rationale for promoting learning organisation approaches, such as mentoring or learning sets. These approaches embed learning beyond isolated training where continuing professional development is often viewed as a staff obligation to fulfil organisational requirements and is experienced as little more than a tick box exercise (Pedler, Burgoyne and Boydell, 1996: 12). This criticism of training and its capacity for transfer and embedding within practice once training is complete has become a significant factor in research and studies supporting learning organisational approaches (Senge, 1990; Day, 1999 in Evans, 2008: 30).

Within this second circle of learning, which has organisation-led opportunities in one half and practitioner-led opportunities in the other, the individual may be able to develop considerable educational capital. This occurs through structured opportunities from both the perspective of practice and the organisation, creating a variety of opportunities for professional learning. Depending on the national and local context, including social, cultural, regional and historical differences, these opportunities can be driven by wider agendas, by strategic goals of the employing organisation, or more locally through the practitioner and practice setting. Initiatives around funding English for Speakers of Other Languages (ESOL) learning provide an example of where marked differences in experiencing and responding professionally and organisationally to a national issue have occurred in further education.

Both projects and formal courses bridge the dividing line between the two halves of our model; that is, between the organisation- or policy-led section on one hand and the practitioner-led section on the other. We illustrate it this way in the second circle as both can be driven by wider social and political agendas. In the 1990s, numerous projects promoted specifically as change initiatives were funded to develop teaching and learning pedagogies in higher education. These include, for example, the Fund for Developing Teaching and Learning (FDTL) and Centres for Enhancing Teaching and Learning (CETL). Although providing well-resourced opportunities for professional development, many of these initiatives had only localised impact, and the knowledge that was acquired remained with the champions and project participants. This was exemplified in the evaluation by SQW Group (sqw.co.uk) of the CETL programme in December 2011. The wider professional impact of some of the initiatives has been disappointing.

In spite of the challenges, projects can provide resources and structure that support learning (Colley, James and Dinet, 2007), becoming useful and effective discrete learning spaces (Macdonald and Wisdom, 2002; Stefani, 2011). Similarly, challenges and opportunities exist in formal professional development courses. These often reflect national priorities and requirements, for example accredited postgraduate certificates in further education and for academic practice in higher education. Although benefiting the professional capital of an organisation, training courses can acquire independent standing and develop their own learning momentum, outstripping the impulses from the drivers that initiated them, adding to the professional capital of the individual. This is amply conveyed in the quote below from one postgraduate certificate programme participant:

> *What I have gained is much more than this accreditation; I became part of a great community of learners, shared and learned from them all, was intellectually stimulated and broadened my horizons in finding innovative approaches to teaching and learning.*

The third and final circle within our model focuses on the wider context as an influencer of professional learning. It has a particularly important role because the individual has to engage with it in order to act in the capacity of critical professional. Within this last circle the wider context can offer spaces for learning, in particular through the use of national and thematic networks. It is essential that whilst working in the field of education we become aware of and engage with the policies that shape our practice. This is described by Evans (2008) as 'extended professionalism'. It is not enough to leave the responsibility and decisions to others, who often lack the nuanced knowledge and understanding of teaching and learning. Our understanding of professional capital requires agency and responsibility, both from individuals and from organisations. Critically engaging with, and professionally questioning, policy and educational strategy is part of this wider work. Although we cannot always see the edges of this circle we can always feel the influence on our professional practice. Becoming actively involved in networks, or participating in consultation activities to make one's voice heard, is often prompted by individual concerns, although the agendas and the repercussions may be wider. The individual professional must be able to consider critically the role and influence of, and her/his responsibility and position towards, policy and professional body frameworks. Each of these will directly influence the individual within her/his practice and in the wider organisational setting. Engaging with wider national or international networks or communities of practice enables the individual to inform, critique and develop practice. Seeing the 'bigger picture' is part of being a responsive and responsible professional.

This model, using three circles, conceptualises and helps to unpack the nature of the spaces and structures of professional learning. As such, it makes it possible to purposefully restructure spaces to enable critical professionalism and to change the scope and impact of learning for the professional educator. By seeing it as a whole, in a *Gestalt* sense, spaces, relationships, opportunities and blockages can be examined together, rather than being seen as separate and unconnected. This is more useful and contributes to a sense of agency rather than seeing professional activities in an atomised way that can be characterised as random, individual and without purpose. How we apply those dimensions of professional learning and how we engage the stakeholders identified through the discussion of the model will influence the success and scope of the professional learning spaces that are framed by the model. This will be discussed as we explore the case studies of practice which follow this chapter.

One of the things we propose with this model is a way for managers, for example, to envision learning space as a tool to develop more engaged and confident employees. These spaces are not expensive but can be viewed as targeted and purposeful. In many cases they are already present. It is the way that we use them to develop professional capital that is important, and we suggest our model allows organisations to draw on funds of experience and capital that already exist for both the organisation and individuals to use. Hence, the model enables us to consider how professionals work as individuals within organisations and are shaped by the wider political and policy context. These relationships are dynamic and require a sense of responsibility and agency on the part of both the individual professional educator and the organisation where they work. Critical professionalism is supported by learning which can be formal and informal, can be organised and unstructured, can be face-to-face or networked but is always social, contingent and contextual. By looking at the various interrelationships, expressed by our circles, we are able to view what already exists and what may be developed to provide professional capital for the individual, the organisation and the field of education. The model is based upon several propositions:

1. The first sees the professional as an individual who learns best through social, discursive and reflective processes structured in and around practice.
2. The second argues for progressive structures to support identity creation in a way that reflects role, career stage and personal and professional need. These structures take account of and enable agency or power.
3. The third interrogates what counts as educational knowledge, raising the questions 'whose knowledge?' and 'how it is acquired and developed?'
4. The fourth acknowledges that professional learning is contingent. It is situated within organisations, practices and processes, and in order to be critical has to embrace wider political and professional contexts.
5. The fifth emphasises the necessity for designing purposeful and embedded approaches to professional learning that maximise critical learning opportunities. It is essential to recognise and acknowledge interrelationships between stakeholders, individuals and political and organisational interests.

How professionals learn

As learning is central to our model we will consider it in more detail here. We understand learning, which includes professional learning, to be social, situated and part of the lived world. We agree that it is a process of meaning-making via a dialogic process through which a knowledge of the world is constructed. Professional learning which supports critical professional development needs to be based upon more than simply acquiring new knowledge, more than being trained in new techniques and more than updating bureaucratic procedures. It has to go beyond tacit knowing. Professional learning needs to be engaged, relevant and related to both theory and practice. In other words, learning must be purposive, deliberative and conscious and it must also be shared. By these means knowledge can be exposed, critically appraised and made accessible.

Lave and Wenger (1991) show the relationship of learning to practice within the widely used social practice approach that we draw upon. Their approach argues that learning does not just happen; it is linked to where, how and why we learn:

> *In our view, learning is not merely situated in practice – as it were some independent reifiable process that just happened to be located somewhere; learning is an integral part of generative social practice in the lived-in world.* (Lave and Wenger, 1991: 35).

Lave and Wenger use the concept of legitimate peripheral participation to explain how we acquire knowledge, in our case professional knowledge, through mastery (sic) to become an expert. Whilst we accept that the apprenticeship approach to mastery may not be fully applicable to the knowing of teachers, we appreciate the value of their concept of a socially situated acquisition of knowledge, and it is this that we draw upon. The emphasis of their approach is not on teaching strategy, technique or pedagogy but on an analytical viewpoint of learning. They describe this as a way of understanding learning which enables a distinction to be made between learning and intentional instruction (p. 40). Their approach acknowledges the social aspects of learning, where activities, tasks and understanding are part of broader systems of relationships. These relationships are not seen as static; as Lave and Wenger argue, the person both defines and is defined by these relations. For us this relational view of learning enables agency and participation as part of the construction of professional identity. Indeed Lave and Wenger argue – and we would agree – that 'learning and a sense of identity are inseparable' (p. 115) as they are part of the same phenomenon. This inseparability of professional learning and identity forms the focus of research into dialogic learning by Vloet, Jacobs and Veugelers (2013) and was also the conclusion of a literature review on teacher identity by Beijaard, Meijer and Verloop (2004). Lave and Wenger's work offers important support for our model of professional learning, as does that of Beijaard *et al.* At the same time, we recognise that whilst the overall approach of Lave and Wenger is useful in highlighting the social, relational and situated nature of learning, the apprenticeship model applied to learning in practice is conservative and does not account for power (Illeris, 2002: 179).

There are many different models and theories of learning (see Illeris, 2009 for a useful collection of these), each based upon a view of what learning is and how it occurs. Drawing together the work of others, Illeris (2002) suggests that learning occurs across three dimensions: cognitive, emotional and social. Within his approach, learning takes place through a process of interaction and internalisation across the dimensions; interaction is important, as he argues, so that the three do not operate individually. This perspective, and his explanation of where the main theories of learning are placed in a dimensional triangle of cognition, emotion and social learning, illustrates the interrelationship between these different aspects of learning. For professional learning to be effective it needs to include aspects of thinking, feeling and working with others.

Others who have researched learning in educational settings have also used a social practice approach to understand the complex factors, interactions and dimensions that shape and develop professional practice. The 'Transforming Learning Cultures in Further Education' initiative, part of the large-scale ESRC-funded Teaching and Learning Research Programme (TLRP), developed a learning culture approach to understand teaching and learning as professional practice and professional identity. Learning cultures are defined as the social practices through which people learn supported through learning opportunities (James and Biesta, 2007). This approach was informed by a theory of learning cultures and related a cultural theory of learning which, the authors argue, provided more authentic insights into the complexities and dynamics of teaching and learning (p. 21). By looking at the culturally constructed relationship between teachers and learners this approach enables us to acknowledge that teachers are also learners within learning cultures as they develop their professionalism in a continually changing environment.

If, as we argue, learning, including professional learning, is situated, social, part of the lived world and should include thinking, feeling and interaction with others, we need to consider how to enable this to happen. To do this we will discuss factors that together contribute to effective professional learning. Those which relate to our model are individual, social and collaborative and environmental factors in professional learning.

The individual

The first set of factors focuses on how professionals draw on a concept of who and what the individual teacher is in relation to:

44

- the idea of teachers as being defined by and learning within and through practice;
- the importance of identity and the close association of practice, subject and self.

These factors emphasise motivation and relevance to learning. The motivation to learn may emerge from individual values, role demands or career drivers, but may equally be influenced by the organisation's strategies, culture and wider national policy. Ideally, professional learning should acknowledge the importance of subject or vocational expertise as defined by the sense of 'expertness' that is intrinsic to the idea of a lecturer, tutor or academic.

We accept the notion of the individual as a cultural construct drawing on Barnett, Parry and Coate's model of the self within learning processes (2001) and Bourdieu's discussion of habitus (1998). Therefore, the professional may be strongly influenced in her/his practice by upbringing, prior experience and indeed by the subject context that is her/his specialism or professional practice base. An expert or subject specialist may feel disempowered on becoming a teacher because of the reduction in professional capital as a consequence of returning to novice status (Pill, 2005). This may cause individual dissonance and even create resistance. However, professional bodies and the marketisation of all education sectors means that the individual is required to develop and engage with a new professional identity. Developing a new identity as teacher, academic or tutor requires both time and consolidation (Robson, 2006: 126). It takes time to negotiate identity development alongside the accommodation and familiarisation processes of engaging with a new, and increasingly fast-changing, education environment. In addition, as we discuss earlier, tensions can emerge between the way that the organisation wishes the individual to structure her/his identity, and the way the individual feels that she/he should do so.

Tensions and challenges can emerge as it is not easy to develop individual teachers through engaging them purely with a generic body of 'pedagogic' knowledge. It is not enough simply to train or inculcate new staff in how to teach (Knight, Tait and Yorke, 2006). Rather, the learning and acquisition of teaching expertise is best achieved where the relevance to the subject is highlighted, and where teaching knowledge is linked to practice and supported within disciplines or subjects. Whilst professional learning may incorporate sharing ideas and practice with others, any knowledge gained has to be resituated and reconstructed in relation to individual contexts and practice.

This is evident in postgraduate programmes that allow and create space for both new and experienced developing teachers to apply and relate core pedagogic knowledge to practice. This is done through talk, through assignment tasks and through significant opportunities for work-based learning to reinforce what may be acquired through formal programmes. Learning about and embedding new knowledge often draws on existing knowledge and practice, but requires significant and sometimes uncomfortable change. The work of Meyer and Land (Meyer and Land, 2003, 2005) develops the term 'threshold concepts' to recognise the particular nature of subject knowledge which enables an individual to become a professional. They argue that this process of becoming draws on outside disciplinary knowledge which is often experienced as 'troublesome knowledge'. Others have developed this concept in teaching and learning (Cousin, 2006, 2010; Appleby and Barton, 2012), showing that the liminal space, where existing knowledge is uncertain, supports transformation and deeper levels of understanding, both for knowledge and practice.

Our two factors in how professionals individually learn recognise the importance of informal learning approaches. The importance of learning from doing, from acting and from being in practice can be seen as part of an activity system (Knight, Tait and Yorke, 2006). It is also a core component of the acquisition of artistry (Eisner, 1985) and of acquiring expertise through a process of participation in legitimate professional practice (Lave and Wenger, 1991). Informal learning can either take place in formal situations, such as institutions and workplaces, or it may be as a result of participation in informal and independent networks (Appleby and Hillier, 2011).

In summary, learning has to be made meaningful by being related to subject specialism and by reflecting the identity, role and context of the individual. There are several models and paths to achieving this; Table 2.1 illustrates the broad descriptive categories and theorists associated with them.

The first three categories imply a progression to learning which is based upon the gradual acquisition of skills, expertise and knowledge through engagement with practice. This may follow an apprenticeship model of learning in the workplace, or it may be facilitated through formal means that shift from minimal levels of competence to skilled,

Table 2.1 Overview of existing models of professional learning

1	Novice to Expert	Apprenticeship model: Dreyfus and Dreyfus (1986), Eraut (1994)
2	Technician to Craftsman to Artistry	
3	Apprentice to Journeyman to Mastery	
4	Self to Students	Focus model: Kreber (2004)
5	Tools to Curriculum	
6	Becoming to Growing to Maturing	Developmental model: Gregorc (1973), Fuller (1970)
7	Early Career Phase – Middle Phase – Late Career Phase	

almost unconscious and often creative, flexible performance. In the latter, practice decisions are founded on a wealth of experience and tacit understandings of practice issues and process.

In categories 4 and 5 we see the emergence of a focus model. This implies that professionals, as they learn, may shift from a focus upon what they are doing to increased concern with wider issues and the needs or perspectives of others. This shift may be evidenced where an early teacher may be very concerned with whether what they are is doing right, whereas more experienced practitioners may be less focused on self and their teaching techniques, and more aware of the learning of others.

Categories 6 and 7 contribute to a developmental model. This is more associated with identity and the sense of one's own capability and competence, career phase, or length of experience. The developmental model highlights that whilst being highly experienced and capable, there may be elements of frustration, of boredom – even withdrawal – involved in how professionals learn. Acknowledging this necessitates renewal, refreshing or change in order to sustain high levels of performance.

Any structure for professional learning has therefore to reflect individual shifts in career points and professional learning progression. Alongside this, it is important to consider the notion of doing professional learning: how the individual engages with professional learning and reflection in order to engage in an ongoing development of self and practice. Professional learning with respect to role and function will change as career profiles develop. Billett (2002: 73, 2004) talks about a process of 'always becoming' and says that professional identity is created through the interaction of workplace and individual. Grossman, Hammermas and McDonald (2009: 278) suggest that professional knowledge and identity are 'woven around practices of teaching'. Both concepts suggest that action and practice are a key component for professional learning. Grossman, Hammermas and McDonald (2009: 276) develop this idea further in their discussion of a curriculum for educational practitioners. They suggest that we may need a curriculum built around the 'practice of a profession' as they emphasise a focus on knowledge development, skill development and professional identity. This aligns well with Barnett's model of self, acting and knowledge described earlier.

Finally, we have drawn on Eraut (1994, 2004) for his work on non-formal learning and the value of his insights into how more experienced professionals learn. He highlights the importance of deliberative learning which supports our view that professionals require space for learning and reflection to make tacit knowing more accessible, less implicit and more purposive. In order to draw out the parallels with our model, we have summarised the key points that he proposes for the deliberative process in Figure 2.2. It supports our model of critical professionalism and learning space and is to some extent exemplified by the discussion of professional dialogue which we address next.

Knowledge and its acquisition

A second set of factors for professional learning draws attention to:

- dialogic processes in learning, and the importance of social construction of knowledge with peers;
- the challenge of acquiring tacit knowledge and its articulation as part of a professional body of knowledge.

Firstly, we explore briefly the role of dialogue and discourse for professional learning. One of the most valuable things we have noted in writing this book has been the value of talk. Talk between the authors of the case studies and the writers has been a process of meaning-making as we deconstruct our practice, share ideas and make tacit understandings meaningful through the reconstruction process of discussion around writing.

Within social constructivist paradigms, dialogue is seen as critical to the process of learning and meaning-making. Communities of learn-

Figure 2.2 Diagram adapting Eraut (2004: 261) to show how his deliberative processes fit within a model of critical professional learning

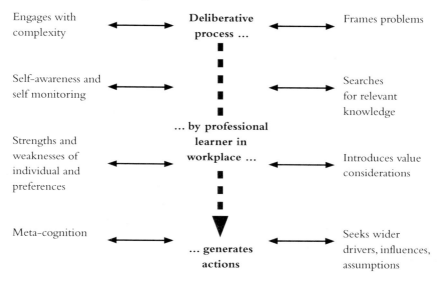

Engages with complexity	**Deliberative process ...**	Frames problems
Self-awareness and self monitoring		Searches for relevant knowledge
Strengths and weaknesses of individual and preferences	**... by professional learner in workplace ...**	Introduces value considerations
Meta-cognition	**... generates actions**	Seeks wider drivers, influences, assumptions

ers in workshops, teams, forums and projects engage in discourse to share understanding and construct a culturally situated 'knowledge base'. In our practice, dialogue facilitates the exploration of practice and theorising around practical knowledge generating discrete, shared or professional knowledge. It allows professional adult learners to share understanding and construct a culturally situated knowledge base. In the work of social constructivists (for example Freire, 1972; Vygotsky, 1978), dialogue plays an important role in the process of learning and meaning-making. It is the central tool for communication, focusing on ensuring that messages sent are received as intended and allowing further exploration of them. The dialogue process in reflection affords benefits by having a different perspective to one's own provided through, for example, a 'critical friend', an objective 'peer', or a 'mentor' (Haigh, 2005). In this way, dialogue in reflective processes leads to greater insight and facilitates the interrogation of assumptions. This is essential for the higher levels of reflection suggested by Habermas (1974), Van Manen (1977), Brookfield (1995) and Larrivee (2008) and is, therefore, a crucial part of professional learning.

Examples of dialogue at work can be seen in peer review of teaching where dialogue is used to help teachers learn (Ho, 2000; Bell, 2001; MacKinnon, 2001; Manouchehri, 2002; Moore and Ash, 2002). It is also used in mentoring and within practicum contexts to expose a learner's conscious competence (Race, 2004) in performance of tasks and interventions. As such, dialogue can effectively be used for the support of reflection on placements and experiential learning (Boud and Falchikov, 2007; Pilkington, 2011a, 2013). It is central to mentoring and coaching techniques (Brockbank and McGill, 1998; Heron, 1999) and has been developed usefully as a reflective and organisational learning tool by Pedler (1996), Laurillard (1999), Ghaye *et al.* (2008) and others. In many teacher training programmes the dialogic process enables peers to generate deep learning together. This provides a valuable contribution of ideas and new perspectives to practise: it is meaning-making through professional talk (Cunningham, 2008). The value of dialogue for processes of academic socialisation and academic literacy building is highlighted as dialogue sits centrally within the process of cultural and individual learning, often being the method of choice for learning within organisational contexts. In organisational contexts, the value of dialogue for supporting experiential learning and change is well established (Reynolds and Vince, 2004), and in education it is recognised for its function in promoting and supporting disciplinary knowledge-formation and cultural development (Becher and Trowler, 2001).

In considering how professionals learn, we recognise the importance of reflective practice: to learn from and in practice. This is supported by critical reflection, conceptualisation and theorising. According to Van Manen (1977) meta-understanding, using conceptualisation and theory, requires the ability and capacity to stand back, interrogate assumptions and explore practice issues informed by theory. This is a skill which can be learned but is also enacted within social contexts and learning spaces. In their exploration of professional learning of teachers in higher education, Knight *et al.* associate professional learning with doing and being; both within an activity system (2006: 324). This, for them, indicates that action in the context of professional learning for educators is an active process strongly allied with an opportunity to learn from and through work. It suggests professionals have to be active in learning, proactive in their approach and not reactive. It requires inhabiting the professional world actively with agency rather than being a passive recipient of it.

The idea of activity, or action, is echoed by Barnett, Parry and Coate (2001) who suggest that in the curriculum for professional subjects the action domain is the most significant. This is clearly of interest to our exploration of critical professional development. They argue, further, that what is required to operate as an informed professional is different within the domains of the arts and humanities and science and technology, as well as in professional subjects. By focusing on the curriculum in this way, they illustrate effectively that critical professional agency is both relational and contingent, operating in differing sites, discourses and communities of practice and power.

Dialogue, therefore, is a central vehicle for learning within and around practice. It enables individuals to explore issues with peers, solve problems, reflect and unpack significant incidents, and exchange ideas. Professional learning using dialogue occurs through conversation with others in the workplace, complemented by workshops and conference participation (Knight, Tait and Yorke, 2006). As professionals learn effectively through consulting others, through dialogue within teams and by social, contextually situated learning, this reinforces the importance of reflective processes and community for professional learning. The discussion of reflection in Chapter One describes how the individual professional takes a socially constructed approach to knowledge acquisition, and how the individual constructs her/his learning through a dialogic process with self and peers and in a dialogue between theory and practice. There are, however, issues with the ways in which communities themselves can generate a discrete, public body of knowledge, although Beijaard, Meijer and Verloop's exploration of teacher identity offers a way of achieving this in their representation of professional identity formation using a teacher's knowledge perspective (2004: 124) This proposes four ways for personal knowledge to become accessible as evidenced in the literature:

- personal knowledge made public through telling and narrative;
- research-based knowledge of teaching;
- personal practical knowledge made conscious through self-reflection;
- personal practical knowledge which remains tacit or unarticulated but is shared by collective experience.

Professionals learn through an ongoing, often unconscious dialogue between practice and theory. This may involve internal theorisation about what works and what doesn't, culminating in the development of expert knowledge. This may be sufficient in stable, albeit complex, environments. However, what currently prevails within both higher and further education, making this more difficult, is a situation of super-complexity and change, particularly in relation to 'client satisfaction' and entrepreneurialism (Barnett, 2008: 192).

The swampy lowlands of practice have become an unpredictable and turbulent sea. In this environment, theory and the learning of others provides an essential means of enhancing the individual's situated, practice-derived knowledge. Learning through dialogue with others in facilitated environments, in work-based opportunities and in events becomes essential. Scholarship and critical interrogation of the individual's practice-derived knowledge becomes necessary for innovation, creativity and problem-solving. This is in addition to simply dealing effectively with the complex currents of policy and educational strategy and the demands of new learners and learning environments. To support this, dialogue works to help professionals learn and synthesise evidence-based theory and scholarship with internal knowledge maps. This is particularly apparent in professional education programmes and in effective work-based learning processes. For example, we have found that participants repeatedly and consistently comment on the benefits of sharing and 'talking' with peers to their learning on formal courses. Networking and learning from peers is a significant professional benefit of the forums, group events, conferences and meetings with which we are involved. Evaluation of courses and events that we organise consistently shows the real benefit of meeting, talking and sharing ideas.

In sum, the critical interrogation of evidence-based theory and practice has acquired a fundamental and essential role within professional learning. It is enacted through dialogic processes. It offers a means of sharing knowledge within the professional community and of enabling the interrogation of explicit learning and teaching theories in relation to subject-specific priorities. This informs our model for critical professionalism.

Learners and learning environments

Here we identify some final points in relation to professional learning that informs our model. These relate to the skills and preferences of the learner and the environment for professional learning focusing on:

- the need to consider the learner role and perspective;
- the environment for learning, its construction and development.

Professional learning can take place across a number of contexts, from formal structured courses and programmes through to learning primarily in the workplace. There is an ongoing debate about which environment achieves most short- or long-terms gains for the individual and for the organisation. Workplace learning is generally acknowledged to be most effective and most relevant to the learning of practitioners, particularly in education (Boud and Walker, 1990; Boud, 1999, 2010). Rather than a simple dichotomy, creating an 'either/or' situation, we suggest that it is important to provide an element of choice that takes account of individual preferences and contextual opportunities such as location, timing and type of delivery. Individual learners will differ as to what learning choice suits them best – a classroom environment, peer support or individual, self-led learning – and the choices made will potentially have an impact upon motivation and achievement. Professional learners are arguably not so different in this respect to those we teach. As well as taking account of environmental and pedagogical factors it is important to recognise an individual's prior learning experience and level of existing skills. A 'one size fits all' approach may be boring and not challenging for experienced learners and may be too detailed for others who are less experienced. As in any teaching it is important to consider differentiation as the skilled independent learner may make the most of workplace learning or any structured learning situation; someone who is less skilled may learn best within a more structured, directed and formal learning environment.

We have found that despite the expertise of the individual, which is always a priority for employment within both higher education and further education, many practitioners may not be skilled at learning. As professional entry routes are varied (and changeable, as discussed in Chapter One) individuals in the higher education or further education workforce may not have meta-learning and learning literacy in respect of teaching and learning. These are skills and learning experiences which make conceptualisation of learning in pedagogic terms more familiar and understandable, providing a basis on which to develop new, and critique existing, knowledge. This may be acquired through ad hoc learning that takes place almost incidentally and unintentionally, or equally it may be part of learning that is directed, targeted and intentional. It is a combination of the environment for learning and the motivation of the learner which results in the type, level and relevance of any learning that occurs.

Learning rarely 'just happens', and critical learning for professional development is even less likely to happen by chance or as an unintended consequence. This type of learning, as we describe in our model, relies upon structures and spaces as well as motivation and opportunity. It is deliberative and purposeful even when informal and non-structured. We use the terms 'enabling structures' and 'learning spaces' to explore this in more detail.

Professional enabling structures and learning spaces

Throughout the book we talk about learning spaces and structures for learning. We define them as spaces and structures which can be temporal, physical or virtual in which practitioners can step aside from work to reflect on and inform their knowledge and learning about practice. Colley, James and Dinet (2007) suggest four principles as a conclusion to their exploration of professional participation for teachers. These recommend 'creating time and space for practitioners to reflect individually and collectively on their work and to develop their professionality' (p. 285). This is a frequent message from researchers in the field, and chimes with our discussion of professional learning spaces and enabling structures.

We consider learning spaces to include:

- ad hoc reflection and dialogue between colleagues about practice;
- learning that emerges in structured reflection and talk with peers on a professional development programme;
- a forum in which educators with shared interests can explore issues of practice and scholarship;
- directed study and reflection on a course;
- organisational, discretely defined space in the form of projects

where peers can collaboratively share and develop initiatives and ideas associated with practice.

In each case we are setting apart a space focused on shared concerns and common interests. Our model identifies workshops and courses, projects, networks, groups and forums at organisational level, as well as for application at wider levels of the discipline, nationally, and even in virtual arenas. Within our model the spaces we propose are often structured or managed by a guide, mentor or facilitator – perhaps an academic developer or practice educator who can provide input, a framework and focus for learning. In this way learning can be supported and become more purposeful. Learning can, of course, occur outside structured or supported spaces (see for example the discussion in Appleby and Hillier, 2011), however, it is more difficult for the outcomes of this learning to be organisationally embedded. To do this an individual needs to understand at a critical level how the spaces, agendas and practice are influenced and inter-relate. This is part of a process of meta-discussion that uses the conceptual tools of critical professionalism and professional capital.

Part of the challenge of designing learning spaces is to ensure that they support and reflect the needs of the individual at particular stages of her/his career and development. It is important to ensure that reflective spaces enable the practitioner to stand back, consider and gain perspective or interrogate assumptions. The influences may be differently perceived, the motivations and choice of space individually driven, and the career stage may affect where the practitioner directs her/his attention and energies. Managers, programme leaders and lecturers will have different roles and responsibilities although they may share a common professional ethic or even a shared vision of the future.

Knowledge is key with respect to how we formulate learning spaces. A learning space has to reflect and recognise the particular nature of educational knowledge. It needs to acknowledge that knowledge in the field of educational practice is broad and messy; it also changes as the individual progresses. This must be reflected within learning spaces when supporting and constructing professional learning about education that acknowledges the complexity of the system and the public discourses surrounding it. Lynn Davies (2004: 211) argues for the need to include an analysis of democracy when questioning how change can be made within education systems to rules, procedures, cultures and leaders. For her, critical analysis of education as a global as well as national complex system can lead to adopting what she calls interruptive democracy. This has four key elements: handling identity and fear; deliberation and dialogue; creativity, play and humour; and defiant agency (p. 212). What this shows is that the type of knowledge within the space is key to the process of learning. For learning spaces to support agency they need to be critical, current and theoretically informed.

There are challenges and tensions between spaces and structures that support individual critical professional development and those that are institutionally organised. The types of organisations that professionals are working in may have structures within the working day that enable professional learning to take place. This may be, for example, a staff room or lunch hour which enables dialogue and exchange; in other words, an ad hoc informal learning space. In further education, the Institute for Learning (IfL) requirement for 30 hours of continuing professional development ostensibly generated space for professional learning. However, the learning encouraged by institutions within this initiative was often technicist and managerialist in its focus and unpopular (Lucas, Nasta and Rogers, 2012). As discussed earlier, this requirement is to be removed, leading to concern over what will take its place. Within many educational institutions, working practices that encourage learning and the existence of physical, organisational learning spaces have been or are being eroded. Lecturers and tutors are increasingly isolated by time and market requirements, in what Ball (2003) describes as the 'terrors of performativity'. This, and what he terms an 'epidemic of reform' (p. 215), prevents the sharing of practice and learning; many of the enabling structures and spaces such as lunch time or common rooms have gone. Within our model, and to counter to these trends, we argue that there are mutual benefits in re-creating spaces for professionals to learn. However, in order to generate these spaces, organisations have to recognise how professionals learn most effectively and to structure learning spaces accordingly.

This is not to suggest that we go back to an imagined 'golden age' of old ideas of professionalism of long reflective summers and lengthy processes of consultation and course design. As many commentators show, this is a myth (Crook, 2008; Evans, 2008), and the current context for education would not allow it. However, we do need to provide opportunities and processes that can be purposefully designed and facilitated to support productive, impactful learning aligned to organisational, practice and professional needs. The next section explores how this might be enabled.

Learning spaces and communities

We have established that professionals need:

- a social context to engage in learning;
- dialogic opportunities and to engage in practice learning with peers;
- reflective space to be able to make meaning and sense of practice and learning;
- organisational space that recognises professional learning is processual, situated and contingent.

The working environment in higher and further education is, however, not an easy place to implement these ideas as it is under pressure, dominated by repetitive and bureaucratic tasks, time-poor and often managerialist. There is a huge demand on the ways that the individual prioritises time and workload in an environment that can be highly charged politically, whilst also strongly affected by national policy. The consequence of this is that, in order for learning and development to take place, there has to be an allocation of resources, time and physical space, and even recognition of the value of learning space. Drawing on the idea of learning organisations is helpful and Lyle (2012), for example, suggests three characteristics for learning organisations which we feel resonate well with what we are proposing. These relate to our concept of learning spaces and the fit of professional capital with the needs of educational institutions within the changed, more dynamic and competitive environment. A learning organisation according to Lyle (p. 218):

1. develops both individual and collective knowledge – which we suggest requires space and time;
2. uses learning to improve performance and competitive advantage – this may potentially be interpreted from a functionalist perspective, but we interpret it in terms of professional capital and a recognition that the nature of professional work is potentially autonomous;

3. continuously enhances its capacity through reflexive praxis to adapt to its external environment – this fits with Ball's view of teachers as producers and embraces our suggestion for critical professionalism, as teachers are the primary producers and therefore must be the locus for change and responsiveness to the environment and needs of learners.

It is necessary to generate environments in a variety of forms that can frame space for learning, reflection and development. Where these environments also align with (organisational) priorities and strategies, they are described as generating expansive learning with the potential for learning that benefits the organisation, the individual and her/his practice (Fuller and Unwin, 2004).

Communities, as we have discussed earlier, are important spaces for professional learning to take place. Whilst recognising their value, we question the validity of communities of practice for the critical professional. For us the concept conveys an idea of acceptance and absorption rather than criticality and agency. It suggests acceptance of the status quo, or at the least the acceptance of the practices of the local subject or discipline setting. Roberts (2006) argues that the relationship between the individual and organisation is not adequately explored in this approach so that the 'boundaries of a community of practice may not reflect organizational boundaries' (p. 636). What constitutes a community of practice is equally open to interpretation, as Becher and Trowler (2001) highlight in their discussion of academic tribes and the influence of a specific discipline's culture. This can be inhibiting and restrictive for the individual, potentially limiting their access and acceptance. Therefore one of the challenges for initial professional education of teachers in higher and further education is to ensure that participants acquire the confidence to challenge the status quo and the 'way-things-are-done', to promote innovation and informed educational practice. The role of the critical professional is to stand back and interrogate practice and assumptions and their sources, as built up through habitual and accepted behaviours and approaches. It is also to make decisions based on what makes good learning rather than what is accepted by others, even in the same professional community of practice.

Communities of practice are often interpreted unproblematically in a flexible and organic way as communities whose membership emerges around a shared interest or concern and a need to share knowledge and practice across the community. This is an uncritical model of communities of practice which is often promoted within organisational and business approaches, alongside suggestions that the organisation can potentially support and encourage the development of communities to engender creative spaces and fulfil strategic need (Wenger and Snyder, 2000). Whilst this could be attractive and serve our requirements for professional learning in that it provides learning space, it is likely that this may constrain the critical professional: by actually accepting the support, the individual may lose autonomy and ownership, or the individual might lose her/his voice. Learning spaces such as these may provide opportunities but may also restrict or constrain them, especially where an individual gives up ownership or becomes subject to other requirements.

Communities may not necessarily be sustainable as the original motivation for the community to exist may dissipate as membership or agendas change (Roberts, 2006). Roberts argues that such communities are not effective, as where managerialism is rife it impedes trust, and the predispositions (habitus) of the individual members may result in tensions. This may be particularly the case in academic settings where individual rather than group or collaborative performance is strongly promoted. Roberts suggests that 'collectivities of practice' (Lindkvist, 2005) may be more appropriate, as they rely on individual knowledge, agency and goal-directed interactions. This suggests that such environments will support learning that is more focused and defined by the participants' interests, rather than by external constraints or agendas. The idea of collectivities of practice may offer a more appropriate model for critical professionals to learn in and adopt as they emerge and function as a result of the engagement and purposes of individual participants. Collectivities of practice also emerge around short- or long-term projects which provide resources and hence discrete structures and enabling space where professionals can learn. Communities and social learning underpin the spaces we propose within our model.

Despite some of the challenges and potential restrictions, groups and communities can act as learning spaces even where they are not necessarily linked to professional learning. Wenger and Snyder (2000) define a range of different groups and their purposes, each of which could potentially act as a learning space (p. 142). They differentiate formal working groups, project teams, informal networks and communities of practice. Groups may vary by membership and lifespan, as well as purpose, and may be either organisationally defined or group-defined, but in each case the community that emerges can act as a learning space.

In contrast, Knight, Tait and Yorke (2006) discuss the broader use of workplace environments to support learning for professional educators. They prioritise considerations that rely less upon the setting and more upon the needs of the professional learners. They emphasise that such spaces need to maximise opportunity for the creation of shared meaning by encouraging collegiality and participation that captures tacit knowledge which can be codified and shared. This is something we have noted as being a particular challenge of communities of practice and also as being particularly desirable given the individualised learning of professional educators within post-compulsory environments. Knight *et al.* argue that such spaces need to have educational validity and purpose, such as a focus on the student experience. So, whilst they share some characteristics of communities of practice they are very clearly focused around educational purposes and values. Knight *et al.* recommend the development of learning teams and learning departments, emphasising the social and collaborative aspects of professional learning.

To this list of community environments or spaces for learning, we can add appreciative inquiry. Tony Ghaye developed this idea by proposing its use to structure specific, targeted space for participative and reflective inquiry. The appreciative nature of the approach he developed means that it does not become imbued with internal agendas or organisational problem-solving but can be viewed as a more creative, positive and proactive tool for development and change (Ghaye *et al.*, 2008). This approach has been adopted within research circles as a means for exploring issues that may be fraught with power and ethical issues, or for researching in organisations. Participatory and appreciative action and reflection (PAAR), as it is called, offers a mechanism that is built around reflection and is therefore appropriate within teaching contexts. It is also orientated towards positive change and development as a group process.

More broadly, learning spaces can be generated and supported through structured peer dialogue, for example within learning sets, discussion groups and reading groups. Learning spaces can also be developed within problem-solving teams, projects and forums. The characteristics of these are that they focus on workplace activities, encourage collaborative and peer working, support reflective practices and are intentional and directed. These characteristics can be seen in the examples that follow, taken from our practice.

Examples of communities as learning space:

1. **A subject team adopts a reflective and peer-centred approach to curriculum design.** The team has the benefit of a shared office and has scheduled regular team meetings and end-of-year reflective events to undertake participatory and reflective curriculum review and redesign. The outcome has been a series of creative and innovative courses focused on community learning and leadership in which the theories they expound have been applied in practice by the team.

2. **A cross-university forum acts to support progressive participation by participants in pedagogic research.** The forum is chaired and resourced centrally, but provides a network of resources and regular meetings through which participants can sustain their involvement and develop their understanding and engagement with pedagogic research. It uses reading groups, paper presentations, seminars, exchanges, conferences and an in-house publication. The network is informal but shared interests bring colleagues together for joint bids for funding, and individual interests are served through events and use of resources.

3. **Rationalisation on a programme can bring about an opportunity for professional learning benefit.** Staff members from different colleges on a course were drawn together at a single delivery hub because of rescheduling. The outcome was that the two groups and an infill group formed a large learning community in which the subject of the course became a catalyst for sharing. Although the amount of facilitation at the start was significant, towards the end the group recognised the value of learning with and from colleagues across diverse institutions.

4. **An initial postgraduate certificate in teaching draws participants from across an institution.** Participants find the value of sharing across a wider community is enhanced through formal tools such as action learning sets and reflective blogs. In addition, peer observing is encouraged reinforcing learning, moving participants out of subject 'silos', helping reflection, and providing affirmation of practice and ideas from others across disciplines. One of the things participants regret at the end of the course is the loss of the community.

5. **A national project explores transferable skills development in language learning.** This project used regular meetings, project tasks and funded time to support the development of a national team. The team shared experience and expertise around a common practice goal. Upon completion, individuals were able to embed new knowledge and skills in practice in the local setting whilst also retaining a loose sense of community built upon trust and the experience of working together.

Enabling structures

In each of the above examples the learning spaces created are situated within the everyday practices of the workplace. They are focused by specific activities, such as course and programme design, planning and review, or enhanced within workshops, forums, working groups and formally structured continuing professional education. Each environment becomes a formally or informally constituted learning space, where the individual can step back from practice to reflect and learn. Fundamental to the development of the critical professional, however, is the learning space that is facilitated and directed. In this way the individual can acquire perspective and distance and engage in meta-learning that empowers and supports agency, or allows the individual to critically engage with the tensions of the conflicting discourses surrounding practice.

The process of engaging with discourse is particularly significant for critical professional learning and contributes to the effectiveness and awareness-building around professional capital for the individual. The individual needs to function effectively within a variety of communities such as the organisational, the discipline or field, and those of research and teaching. Each of these is a system with its own literacies and practices. Beyond this there are political and strategic imperatives that can generate additional discourses and communities with which the critical professional may wish to align. Within this supercomplex and dynamic educational setting, professionals make choices about where to locate themselves and how to professionally identify themselves and direct their energy. This is a discursive process that Barnett suggests is central to professionalism: the 'achievement of professionalism lies in discursive (self) creation' (in Cunningham, 2008: 190). For us, the crucial component is the purposeful structuring of facilitative learning spaces. In examining practice we can identify several spaces and enabling structures that

62

emerge as potential dialogic learning spaces within workplace settings and processes. These are organised in Table 2.2 as activities related to teaching, general activities and peer-supported activities.

Each of the environments and activities can be purposefully structured to direct the learning of the professional. This may be as the result of organisational, strategic or individual effort. Their success, however, rests largely on the dialogue process that takes place within them or, perhaps more valuably, around them in order to draw out the reflective potential for the individual. This is made particularly powerful through targeted scaffolding using critical reflection and around critical incident analysis, or through mentored and facilitated professional dialogue. These all require intervention and skilled support and structured space. As we argue earlier, learning doesn't just happen. Formal professional education, as in courses, programmes and events, can provide structured space and also the opportunity for dialogue, including the wider perspective and critique that supports critical professionalism. However, there are numerous organisational processes that can be made to act as structured learning space. It is the reflective, dialogic and directed process within the learning space that achieves this criticality and perspective, and which can be applied creatively in differing contexts. This will be discussed in more detail in the case studies and in the final chapter.

Learning spaces can, therefore, be widely interpreted as formal, structured, dialogic, reflective, organisational and practitioner-based. The learning spaces can be physical, temporal or virtual. The key is that they are facilitated and facilitative, framing the dialogue and the development

Table 2.2 Enabling structures and learning spaces in workplace settings

Activities related to teaching	General activities	Peer-supported activities
Course leadership	Administration, boards	Mentoring
Course development committee	Research groups	Shadowing
	Projects	On-the job learning
Programme review	Meetings, forums	Observation
External examining	Conferences	Peer review
Module leadership	Workshops	Action learning sets
Quality review	Networks	
Moderation		

of the individual. The individual needs structure and time to reflect even with critical incidents, so enabling structures and learning spaces may be structured around either time or around process. They may be framed within the organisational systems and activities, or within individual requirements, however the purpose of engaging in critical professional development remains a central organising feature.

Part Two

Examples in practice

Introduction to Part Two

The case study section focuses on examples of practitioners creating learning spaces and enabling structures. It provides the evidence based in practice that supports our proposal for learning spaces and enabling structures in critical professional development. There are four case studies drawn from our own practice and that of colleagues targeting different sectors. Each illustrates different aspects of the model described previously, showing how spaces have been structured and targeted. The case studies demonstrate how particular facets of our definition for critical professionalism can be understood in practice, providing a basis through which the model can be deconstructed, applied and interpreted in a range of organisations and contexts.

The first case study, in Chapter Three, describes how a programme can structure the support for a newly emerging professional group – in this case, deaf and British Sign Language (BSL) teachers. Lynne Barnes describes the delivery of an externally accredited award for deaf and BSL teachers which provides recognition of existing skills and a professional career structure where previously none had existed. The second case study, in Chapter Four, focuses on creating enabling structures within an organisation. Ruth Pilkington describes how a series of courses can develop the 'scholarly practitioner', beginning with initial education and concluding at doctoral level. This work is part of a structured professional framework for educators, enabling critical professional development through practitioner research and scholarly activity. In the third case study, in Chapter Five, Christine Hough describes her work with undergraduates studying early years' education largely part-time.

She discusses the ways that students of this vocational subject can be supported, through structured activity, in acquiring critical professional skills and confidence, enabling them to influence change within the workplace setting. The final case study adapts the approach of the first three case studies more flexibly. In Chapter Six, Yvon Appleby focuses on communities as learning space. Using three short case studies she explores examples of writing for professional development. Each example is described and discussed to show how writing communities can support the development of academic and scholarly practice and confidence.

The third part of the book, which follows these case studies, will analyse each example in relation to our model of critical professional development. This will support a final, more detailed discussion of how spaces and structures can be employed to support professional development to benefit the capital of both individuals and organisations.

CHAPTER THREE

Developing critical practice in non-traditional learners: Training deaf people to teach

Lynne Barnes

Introduction

Teacher training for those wishing to teach British Sign Language (BSL) has, historically, been largely neglected. Training courses designed specifically for BSL teachers are scarce and often provided on a piece-meal basis. However, generic teacher training courses do not meet the pedagogic needs of BSL teachers, who are in the main native BSL users with non-traditional academic backgrounds and experience. In 2009, the University of Central Lancashire (UCLan) introduced a British Sign Language teacher training course that was designed specifically to meet the needs of deaf learners. Delivered entirely in BSL, the students were able to access the curriculum in their first language, rather than via an interpreter. This chapter discusses different methodologies for developing BSL teachers as critical practitioners, and explores how these underpin the professionalisation of BSL teaching. It also illustrates how a course/training programme provides space and structure for deaf educators. The programme was prompted by concern that the existing English-language training for deaf BSL teachers was inadequate: although individuals previously managed to obtain some level of qualification to be able to teach British sign language, their own learning experience as a linguistic minority was often limited and isolating. This directly affected their pedagogic development as teachers and, more widely, their professional careers as deaf educators.

Target audience – deaf people as learners

The vast majority of BSL teachers in the United Kingdom are deaf and native BSL users. As a result, they tend to come from non-traditional academic backgrounds and have a limited academic and educational experience. Educational achievement amongst deaf learners falls well short of that of their hearing peers at all levels of education (National Deaf Children's Society, 2008). As well as lower academic achievement, the overall experience of the education system is often emotionally unrewarding and psychologically challenging (DEX, 2003). As a minority group in mainstream society, deaf people generally – and sign language users specifically – often suffer from a lack of positive role models and have a restricted set of career aspirations (Woolfe, 2004). Those who find themselves working as BSL teachers often do so by chance, rather than as a considered career choice (Atherton and Barnes, 2012). Another instance in which BSL teachers find themselves outside standard educational expectations is that they may be expected to teach a subject they have never themselves studied. It may be a surprise to learn that whilst deaf sign language users might on occasion be taught in their native language (although this is far from the norm in the UK), they are almost never taught the language itself. The only test of their language competency comes if they choose to take the communicative assessments offered by various awarding bodies that are designed for hearing students. This does not require them to undertake any study of the language but often simply involves an examination of their communication abilities.

The same principles apply when sign language users are employed to teach BSL in colleges of further education, where the majority of such courses are delivered. For many educational establishments, a level of language competency appears to be a sufficient requirement for teaching BSL, rather than the type of teaching qualifications required for other subjects. This lack of qualification is recognised by those working within the sector: 'The fact that a person is deaf does not automatically mean that they should teach' (Barnes and Padden, 2009: 37).

This leads to many BSL teachers having to learn 'on the job':

> *I remember when I was offered this full-time teaching position I didn't have any teaching qualifications. I only had CACDP Level 1 and 2 [communication skill awards roughly equivalent to GCSE and AS-level]. It was the feedback I got from the students and other*

teachers that helped me develop my teaching skills. (Barnes and Eichmann, 2010: 9)

Not all BSL teachers are unqualified: research shows that some experienced teachers hold a variety of teaching qualifications (Barnes and Eichmann, 2010), ranging from City & Guilds 7307 (part 1) at one end of the spectrum to a postgraduate certificate in education (PGCE) at the other. Less than five per cent of those interviewed held a certificate of education (Cert Ed), whilst 15 per cent had successfully attended the BSL teacher training course offered by Durham University (DUBSLTTC) from 1985 to 1999. From this evidence, two aspects of BSL teacher training become clear: firstly the overwhelming majority do not hold adequate teaching qualifications. The majority of those who do have teaching qualifications have not been trained in language teaching and, more specifically, have not been trained to meet the specific pedagogic challenges of teaching and learning a visual/gestural language. In addition, assessment strategies relevant to learning and knowledge of sign language differ greatly from those suitable for spoken languages. These are never explored in generic teacher training courses and so sign language tutors are left to interpret the written curriculum and examination criteria of the awarding bodies as the basis for their teaching.

The second factor to emerge is that there are clearly ample opportunities open to deaf people to gain teaching qualifications, such as those listed above as well as the more recently introduced PTLLS (Preparing to Teach in the Lifelong Learning Sector), CTLLS (Certificate in Teaching in the Lifelong Learning Sector) and DTLLS (Diploma in Teaching in the Lifelong Learning Sector) awards. However, these courses are neither designed for, nor do they meet, the pedagogic needs of sign language users. Generic courses are delivered in spoken language, with access provided via BSL/English interpreters. Research has shown that when the curriculum is delivered in this format, a significant portion of the content is lost in the interpretation process and the message is decayed. The extent to which filtering of important information occurs is compounded by the skill levels and subject-specific knowledge of the interpreters used on such courses (Harrington and Turner, 2001).

It is inevitable that inaccuracies and misunderstandings occur and that Deaf students often struggle to fully achieve their academic

potential or become fully integrated into the community of learners.
(Harrington, 2000, cited in Mole and Peacock, 2006: 124)

In such settings, sign language users are taking part in a mediated learning environment, and so become effectively second-hand learners through an inability to be immediate and proactive participants in the learning process. Furthermore, their access to and understanding of course content is almost totally dependent on the skills of those providing the interpretation. Freire's concept of banking education offers a model for understanding this lack of engagement, in which they become passive learners at best (Freire, 1972).

> *When I did my A1, it was with a hearing tutor [and] there was no 'connection' with the tutor. From my experience in linguistics and working here, I know that information is usually condensed and reduced when relayed through an interpreter, so it often results in me working out things on my own.* (Barnes and Padden, 2009: 32)

As well as failing to establish a rapport with the tutor, deaf students miss out on the educational benefits of studying within a supportive peer group. Whilst having interpreters present in the classroom might appear to encourage interaction between deaf and hearing students, deaf students often feel isolated amongst hearing students:

> *It seems that deaf people are more isolated within courses, and there's no support network for them. (Ibid.)*

Communication barriers between deaf and hearing students are one cause of this sense of isolation, with students unable to share experiences and discuss issues arising from their studies. This adversely affects interaction and engagement on a number of levels, with an impact on critical discourse and reflective practices between students. A further consequence of communication difficulties between deaf and hearing students is an absence of critical consciousness (Freire, 1972) and a lack of awareness of the different cultural norms of each group of students (DEX, 2003: 47). Feeling isolated can create a loss of self-worth and seriously inhibit the learning process by inculcating a 'culture of silence' (Freire, 1972) amongst deaf students:

> *[On a course with hearing students] I did not have the confidence*
> *to ask questions at the end, as I wasn't sure I had understood things*
> *properly.* (Barnes and Padden, 2009)

Interpreters can be unwitting participants in this process, as deaf students necessarily receive information later than their hearing peers and have fewer opportunities to contribute, discuss and respond within the classroom. An important aspect of having access to a supportive peer group is the opportunities that the group provides to use scaffolding as a teaching and learning strategy. Several researchers have identified scaffolding as a form of dialogue that helps learners to complete a task they could not have managed on their own (Martin, 2005). In the absence of direct interaction with their course tutors, deaf students have a greater need to be part of an effective peer group, as otherwise there is no forum in which this scaffolding can take place. Without deaf peers, deaf students have no opportunity to interact, to develop their ideas and understanding of pedagogy or to share cultural experiences and outlooks.

The ultimate consequence of current teacher training opportunities for sign language users has been the creation of a workforce which is largely underqualified at best and deprofessionalised through no fault of their own. Courses are not tailored to the pedagogic needs of deaf students, in that they do not allow students to establish a rapport or direct dialogue with their tutors or fellow (hearing) students or provide effective scaffolding opportunities. The unique nature of sign language and the visual/gestural modality of its teaching render many of the methodologies employed on generic courses irrelevant to deaf learners wishing to teach the subject. Although some students might complete these courses and gain teaching accreditation as a result, they are often ill equipped as critical practitioners or subject specialists. They have the necessary paperwork, they have the practical language skills, but they have not been trained in the specific pedagogic skills required by sign language teachers.

Creating a learning space – training deaf people to teach

Although there has been no empirical research conducted to identify the pedagogic needs of deaf BSL teachers, these difficulties have long been recognised within the sector. Over the years there have been several attempts to create specific courses for BSL teachers. The most highly regarded of these was the Durham University British Sign Language Teacher Training Course (DUBSLTTC) which was available between 1985 and 1990. This course, delivered by deaf people themselves, produced high-quality teachers who were able to meet the standards necessary for teaching the then Council for the Advancement of Communication with Deaf People national BSL awards. However, this course and others like it were not mapped to the National Qualifications Framework or accredited by the Qualifications and Curriculum Authority. BSL teachers were holding qualifications that were directly relevant to their practice but they were not recognised as qualified teachers. With the demise of these discrete courses by the early 1990s, BSL teachers were left both untrained and unqualified but still able to teach the language in a variety of educational settings. This problematic situation might have continued indefinitely, but the lack of training and adequate qualifications became a serious issue in 2007, when educational reforms required all further education teachers to hold formal qualifications for the first time. It became essential firstly that BSL teachers were made aware of these new qualifications, and secondly, that they were offered practical and appropriate opportunities to gain these awards, which in turn would enhance the status and quality of BSL teaching as a profession.

In an attempt to address this lack of opportunity, the BSL and deaf studies team at the University of Central Lancashire designed and developed a British Sign Language teacher training course. Initially funded by the Department of Children, Schools and Families, as part of the national I-Sign project (I-Sign, 2009) our aim was to provide a course that met the needs of deaf BSL teachers by being delivered solely in BSL, whilst also meeting the requirements of the national framework for teachers in further education. This unique course consists of three modules; the PTLLS, the CTLLS and a continuing professional development module in applied sign linguistics. Together, these modules ensure that, on completion, students are eligible to register with the Institute for Learning (IfL) as associate teachers. These modules provide both the threshold skills for teaching and the essential subject knowledge required for teaching BSL. As the vast majority of BSL teachers follow syllabi and curricula written by national awarding bodies, and assessment is undertaken by representatives of the national awarding body (rather than the teachers themselves), associate teacher status is appropriate in the first instance. We hope to develop a diploma course in the near future but, in the interim, those graduates from our course who wish to further their studies and training have to join DTLLS courses provided by local colleges. Unfortunately, many of these courses replicate the shortcomings for deaf learners that were outlined earlier and so there is still an urgent need for further development of training provision of the type we have pioneered at UCLan.

Discussion

One of the first issues we had to address when designing our course was how and when to deliver it. The number of BSL teachers working locally was too small to provide a full cohort able to attend on a weekly weekday basis. The vast majority of BSL classes are provided by local colleges which employ BSL teachers on a part-time basis and according to demand. Teaching usually takes place at night, with BSL teachers employed elsewhere and in other types of work during the day. A particular consequence of part-time working is the limited support for and availability of staff development and continuing professional development activities. BSL teachers working on a part-time basis are unlikely to be eligible for staff development funding from either of their employers; colleges and other organisations offering BSL classes may be unable or unwilling to invest in developing part-time staff, whilst the teachers' main employers (their 'day jobs') are unlikely to fund staff development that is not directly relevant to their businesses. Students may also need to weigh the high costs of self-funding professional development (potentially £600 for a PTLLS course and £1,000 for a CTLLS course) versus the potential long-term benefits that might accrue from what is, after all, only an insecure part-time income source.

Therefore, we decided on a blended learning approach. Modules were delivered once-monthly on a taught block basis, (Thursdays through to Saturday), and supported by online teaching materials and tutorials. The commitment of students on the course to their professional development, and the appeal of the course itself, are demonstrated by the facts that many of the students travel long distances, pay their own travel and accommodation costs and give up their weekends to engage in this unique career enhancement opportunity. The overriding principle in designing the course was that it should be taught exclusively in BSL so as to provide direct access to the curriculum in the students' first language. In addition, each of the classroom sessions was filmed and made available online, alongside all of the teaching materials. Unable to take notes whilst watching the lecturer or engaging in classroom activity, students were provided with a first-hand record of what had been taught each day. This video served not only as an aide memoire, but could be used as a reference and resource by allowing the students to experience the lectures again at their own speed. An equally important reason for putting these resources online is that teacher training resources in sign language simply do not exist. BSL teachers are forced to rely on standard teacher training manuals and guides in written English. This causes major obstacles for people who do not have English as their first language and who because of their deafness have a language and literacy delay (Rodda and Eleweke, 2000).

The approach we chose to adopt has resulted in many of our students having the unique experience of being first-hand learners, rather than being recipients of teaching that has been filtered through a third party, as represented by BSL/English interpreters. For the first time, teachers of BSL were offered the chance to take part in activities that develop their knowledge and skills in reflective practice, critical thinking, peer observation, self-assessment and the full range of teacher development activities.

Developing critical learners

The skills described above are vital ingredients in producing and maintaining effective educational practitioners, but one element that is particularly lacking amongst deaf learners is the opportunity and ability to engage in critical reflection. The part-time and often solitary nature of BSL teaching, which does not provide any meaningful peer support network within educational settings, coupled with the educational experiences of the teachers themselves as deaf people, means that critical reflection does not normally form any part of BSL teaching skills. Therefore, this next section will focus on the way in which developmental reflection is a core aspect of the BSL teacher training course offered at UCLan.

Developmental reflection is fostered through group discussions amongst the BSL teachers, led by the course tutors. These discussions take a critical discourse approach, with students encouraged to engage in individual and collective analysis of why their experiences affect them;

what they have learnt from taking part in these discussions; why they feel such knowledge exchange is important; how the whole process of reflection helps them develop as learners and then as teachers; and how they utilise this learning in their teaching practice.

The ability to develop reflective skills takes a different form amongst deaf learners, as they require numerous specific and concrete examples that need to be unpacked before more abstract concepts begin to be recognised and understood. Another aspect of deaf learning that differs significantly from that of hearing people is that the students tend to record and discuss the reflections of others before they identify links to their own experiences. Students discuss their experiences in small groups and often marvel at how similar these are amongst peers, especially their shared negative experiences of their own education in mainstream classrooms. The learning gained from these exchanges is then shared with the whole group and video-recorded. Not only do they critically reflect on their own development as learners and teachers, they also learn from each other, support each other in the presentation and delivery of their experience and find comfort in having a peer group whose members have similar experiences to themselves. This ability to share with their peers is both rewarding and unique; in regular teacher training situations, our learners have often been the only deaf person present and are merely passive watchers, via an interpreter, whilst others share mainstream hearing experiences. This has to be taken in the context of deaf BSL users as an 'oppressed' minority group, who have had little or no opportunity to engage with their learning, or even their teachers, who cannot discuss conceptual thoughts about their work with peers in their own language, and who lack the peer support and scaffolding necessary for self-development. On this course, all these issues are addressed and students are no longer afraid to 'get it wrong' because they are amongst others like themselves and therefore do not feel intimidated or suffer from a lack of self-worth that often results from being taught alongside hearing people. In addition, students' individual reflections are presented to the group and captured in digital video format. As these interactions take place in BSL, the problem of using written and spoken English as a tool for assessment is removed, together with the associated pressures on deaf BSL users identified earlier. A further consequence of this approach is that students have an inclusive and equal learning experience that is much more appropriate to the subject they will be teaching.

One aspect of the course that brings together the peer support, mentoring and practical pedagogic elements is the mini-teaching sessions all students have to take part in. Mini-teaching provides students with a unique opportunity to observe and assess their peers, and in many respects this is no different to standard practice on any other teacher training course. Where this proves unique to this course is that students have their first experience of observing a BSL teaching session. For deaf students who enrol on a generic course, such an opportunity is not available. Nor will the majority of BSL teachers have seen a BSL class being taught at any stage of their academic career; indeed, they are highly unlikely to have taken a BSL class as students themselves. The trainee teacher is assessed by both course tutors and fellow students, providing valuable opportunities for reflection, evaluation and feedback, as well as identifying and sharing good practice. The impact of this crucial learning experience for those on the course cannot be overemphasised, as the following quotes from students' unpublished course evaluation reports indicate:

> *It gives me the opportunity to see my strengths and weaknesses and also the chance to observe other students.* (Student A)

> *To see examples of different teaching methods, resources and activities.* (Student B)

> *Constructive feedback helped me to ... improve.* (Student C)

Additional unique elements of this course

There are many aspects of this course that make it unique in terms of both the pedagogy employed and the benefits that accrue to the deaf learners on the course, some of which have already been identified. The course provides a rare opportunity for BSL users to engage in first-hand learning and, in addition, the students are doing so alongside other experienced BSL teachers. This provides an awareness and understanding of the commonality of the issues faced by both themselves and their contemporaries and peers, and this, in turn, acts as a foundation for the students to develop critical reflection skills through an extensive interchange of specific examples of issues they have all faced. From such personal and concrete examples, a greater understanding and awareness of the underlying abstract principles of their teaching practice and experiences can emerge in a way that is not otherwise available to them. Through the exclusive use of BSL as the medium of communication, access to education, the course curriculum and all aspects of the training are delivered directly to the students in their first language.

One of the most important and unique aspects of this course is the creation of a peer support network, which in turn provides a scaffolding framework for what is otherwise little more than a collection of individuals isolated from each other and those they work alongside. Emery (2007) has shown that learning from peers in social and work-based settings contributes to a vibrant learning community amongst deaf people. Benefits derived from this approach include having access to a mutually supportive network and the sharing of ideas, experiences and resources. This helps to mediate the problems of English-based materials that are not appropriate or relevant to BSL teaching and allow students to 'scaffold' their ideas and knowledge (Barnes and Doe, 2007). Within the peer group created by this course, deaf students are able to interact and so develop their ideas and understanding of the pedagogy of BSL teaching. Course tutors and fellow students can also act as mentors to less experienced colleagues, as well as developing as mentors for subsequent cohorts of students on the course and for fellow BSL teachers in their own areas. The lack of mentoring has been highlighted as another major challenge faced by BSL teachers, particularly those working in hearing environments (Barnes and Eichmann, 2010). The mutually supportive nature of the support provided to and by students on the course offers real potential for the continuing development of formal and informal mentoring networks that simply do not exist at the moment.

Outcomes: Deaf people as critical practitioners

There are several notable outcomes of this initiative to develop critical practice in non-traditional learners, through training deaf people to teach. This course has, for the first time, produced teachers of BSL who resemble other teachers in further education by providing an accessible and culturally appropriate route to gaining associate teacher qualification and status. Generic teacher training courses might allow deaf people to qualify as teachers, but they are not provided with the necessary tools and skills to teach BSL. Furthermore, by developing trainees as critical practitioners, the course has introduced achievable professional standards for BSL teachers that meet the expectations of the National Qualifications and the Qualifications and Credit Frameworks.

The course does more than merely train BSL teachers; it serves as a foundation for continuing professional development. Graduates from the course serve as informal mentors to both fellow students and peers already working within the profession. To support this mentoring role, and to publicise the professionalisation agenda for BSL teachers, the course delivery team at UCLan have developed an online resource for those interested in training as BSL teachers. This development has been funded by Learning and Skills Improvement Service and is hosted on the Excellence Gateway (www.excellencegateway.org.uk/bslteachers). A national network of regional BSL teacher networks has also been established, to provide all BSL teachers with access to a peer support network they can draw on for mentoring and career development.

This innovative and ground-breaking course serves as a template for the ongoing process of professionalising BSL teaching in the UK. The course delivery team do not claim this process is complete, but deaf people working as BSL teachers have been given a unique opportunity to develop their critical thinking and reflective practice skills. This has helped to address some of the shortcomings of the profession and respond to the desires of those working as BSL teachers to establish professional standards within the sector.

CHAPTER FOUR

A progression framework for formal continuing professional development

Ruth Pilkington

Introduction

This case study describes a series of courses and awards which colleagues and I have designed to support and structure professional learning for education practitioners. These courses embrace diverse disciplinary approaches to higher and further education, complementing subject specialisms and pedagogies, in order to integrate leadership, scholarship and research in a progression framework. The framework links a series of formally accredited courses providing practitioners in further and higher education with learning spaces and enabling structures for developing themselves as both critical practitioners and academic leaders. Through this suite of professional education courses, we believe we have constituted a means for professionals to come together and learn from each other and to progressively acquire research and scholarly tools for developing their practice.

At the centre of this case study sits the individual, or scholarly practitioner. Practitioner learning begins from practice, from what individuals know, which can be shared and developed through research and scholarship, acquiring a critical perspective. Through this, reflection as part of this process is embedded in a formal accredited course structure and is engaged with more meaningfully through dialogue with others. The result is to generate a more critical and reflexive approach around professional knowledge rather than focusing on self- and problem-solving reflection.

Target audience – the scholarly practitioner

The underlying driver for our courses is the concept of a 'professional educator'. We see the professional educator as being both a subject specialist and an educator – as someone who can act at a level of professional 'artistry' (Schon, 1987) who is critical, reflective and able to develop self and the praxis associated with the subject. The 'professional educator' engages with development of pedagogical understandings through individual research, practitioner inquiry and project activity. This scholarly approach to enhancing practice is described by Yorke (2000) as involving three levels of engagement through which lecturers can engage in research processes:

1. by benefiting from the outcomes of others' research;
2. by collaborating with research activity, though not undertaking research themselves;
3. as active researchers.

We have applied these principles to a course-based approach to professional development, which accommodates the fact that educational practitioners benefit from the communities of practice, discourse and reflection opportunities encompassed in a formal (qualifications) route. It also reflects Boyer's outline with respect to scholarship and research. Following on from Boyer (1990) we regard the development of professionals as a scholarly enterprise in which teaching begins with what the teacher knows: 'Pedagogical procedures must be carefully planned, continuously examined, and relate directly to the subject taught' (p. 23). Hence, we adopt a model of research-informed teaching, where research informs understandings of pedagogy or teaching, formally structured into the progressive programme for participants in the MEd suite of awards outlined below.

Our programmes cover initial professional learning through postgraduate certificates, providing staged progression and development of the practitioner. They build on this with further stages of study, leading to a masters degree (through postgraduate diploma and MEd) consolidating research into practice (Healey and Jackson, 2004). The final stage involves completing a professional doctorate (EdD), through which the practitioner acquires and demonstrates professional leadership and expertise making a contribution to original professional knowledge.

The flexible structure of our programmes supports continuing professional development and develops a number of elements: criticality, inquiry, rigour, a reflective and reflexive stance, enhancement of practice, methods for researching practice, and professionalism. The programme is underpinned within our framework by concepts of dialogue as well as notions of collaborative meaning-making and exchange (Pilkington, 2011). For us, enabling sharing, learning and reflection is important because it is respectful of the needs of professionals, the higher education environment and the primacy of the discipline. As a result I feel we have designed a structure that can meet the needs of a wide range of educational professionals in a wide range of settings. In the next section I relate the route taken to develop our awards, explaining how we have embraced and benefited from this diversity.

The enabling structure – the MEd progression framework

The route to the MEd began in 2003. I was still relatively new in my own role as course leader of an initial professional education programme for higher education staff at the university, the postgraduate certificate in learning and teaching in higher education (LTHE). This course provides accredited initial professional status for higher education academics similar to the role played by a secondary postgraduate certificate in education and post-compulsory postgraduate certificate in further education (PGCFE). The course had been freshly validated and recognised by the professional bodies, the Staff and Educational Development Association (SEDA) and the Institute for Learning and Teaching in Higher Education (ILTHE), a forerunner of the HE Academy. I was interested in ways of supporting professional development beyond, and complementary to, the postgraduate certificate in LTHE. Participants gained so much from the exchanges and community of the course and I wanted to replicate this for continuing professional development purposes. I had already been working with colleagues on sister awards for researchers and e-learning but I experienced a 'eureka' moment whilst attending a SEDA conference which profoundly influenced my development of the MEd.

The SEDA Professional Development Framework was just being launched (see www.seda.ac.uk/professional-development). It prompted me to envisage a formal framework of accredited modules and awards that could structure continuing professional development for higher education staff across the university, building on the postgraduate certificates I was co-ordinating. I was caught up by the vision of allowing individuals to progressively develop skills and knowledge around their roles, functions and needs, culminating in a masters degree in professional practice in education (MEd) (Pilkington, 2004).

The MEd that emerged took as its starting point a series of postgraduate certificates such as the postgraduate certificate in LTHE, which focuses on front-line, technical and pedagogic skills and initial competence. Through completing the postgraduate certificate in LTHE, individuals acquire professional competence and the knowledge, capacity and skills to function as active members of the educational community. Applying Kreber's model of professional learning (2004), this means that the individual may be effective and competent at this stage at a pedagogic level with some curricular level expertise. By progressing through from the certificate to the postgraduate diploma the professional can develop advanced levels of competence by building areas of expertise, and by broadening perspectives on practice so as to acquire criticality. This is managed using individual modules within the postgraduate diploma stage. Practitioners choose from a range of individual modules that support ongoing continuing professional development and deepening of engagement in practice. The MEd progressively builds on the idea of competence so that on completion of the Masters award, the individual has developed practice expertise enhanced through applied research and educational inquiry. The individual will also have acquired the capacity for contributing to leading and developing the profession, and for the generation of new professional knowledge. In this way the course simultaneously responds to ideas of teacher knowledge and development (Shulman, 1987) and engagement in communities of practice.

It is interesting to see the benefits of a programme like this with participants drawn from several sectors and disciplines learning from and with each other. I have observed participants on modules generate genuine energy; for example, in networking events associated with the awards in class and during module action learning sets (Pedler, 1996) and workshops. Modules in particular appear to generate safe, reflective collegial environments for discussion and sharing, allowing professionals to learn from each other, using common generic topics enriched by the different perspectives of the varied subject cultures.

In 2006 we redesigned the MEd to embrace wider routes for access on to this developmental structure. The university has a strong regional net-

84

work of colleges using the postgraduate certificate in further education, and the postgraduate diploma modules were adopted and later enhanced to meet the needs of colleagues by designing a specific progression route for college staff. Their initial professional education (PGCFE) was provided within colleges by local educational developers, then taken further by university staff delivering extension modules at college 'hubs' using evening delivery. At the MEd stage, higher, further and increasing numbers of lifelong learning and other educational practitioners all come together at the university site to complete a practitioner research project. This diverse community is supported using workshops and learning sets, resulting in lively and genuine exchange across the sectors. The sense of community has been further strengthened through an annual 'sharing practice conference' which is regionally based and uses poster presentations to maximise discussion and sharing.

Modules are developed around a set of principles, and individual modules enable practitioners to focus attention around their own development. The principles include:

- learning for teachers and academics which begins with practice and focuses on practice;
- a notion of the 'reflective practitioner', learning from experience but informed by scholarly engagement with literatures;
- a model for engagement with scholarly practice that acknowledges the dual professional nature of the lecturer: subject specialism and a 'professional stance' towards developing and enhancing teaching and learning practice;
- provision of communities that support the development of the professional within subject fields and across wider communities;
- support for increased criticality and reflective engagement with teaching and learning research;
- an acknowledgement that individual practitioners need to engage with appropriate methods and approaches for learning about how to research teaching and learning: action research, qualitative paradigms, ethical and power considerations, practitioner research, and reflexivity.

Modules might focus on leadership, personal development, research skills or teaching development, or enhancement of particular areas of skills, knowledge or practice. The modules are conceived around the idea of a practitioner committed to professional values, through work-based learning informed by scholarship and ultimately research. Examples of modules include curriculum design, innovative teaching, critical professionalism, research methods, professional writing and leadership. They all use work-based assignments and reflective discourse within classes to support learning in a structured way.

Within the course, key modules focus on developing the academic practitioner and show engagement with ideas of criticality and the scholarly and informed practitioner in their design. These modules are as follows:

1. At postgraduate certificate level, there is a 20-credit, Level 7 module on 'enhancing professional practice'. This uses a piece of secondary inquiry to encourage the practitioner to engage critically with literature and to benefit from the 'outcomes of others' research' (Yorke, 2000) to inform an inquiry into a problem or issue they have in their practice. This inquiry often leads to further application and development in practice. In tracking careers from the postgraduate certificate, we have seen former participants gain awards for teaching and learning excellence for innovation; participants obtaining project funding for their practice; participants who have continued to study teaching and learning through completion of the MEd; and finally, we have seen numerous articles emerge.

2. At postgraduate diploma level there are five research-oriented modules, including a module on action research, and a further module called 'the Critical Professional'. These develop research skills and familiarity with educational research approaches and methods, but also encourage critical perspectives on literature and others' research (Stierer and Antoniou, 2004; Brew, 2010).

3. The module on the Critical Professional has a particularly important role to play in developing the capacity and capability of our participants to engage in critical reflection and scholarly practice. It builds on notions of professional practice which recognise that practitioners develop through critical reflection on practice informed by:

   a. a wider understanding of their context, policy and influences on practice, which shifts the attention of the professional from technical classroom-focused practice to one that embraces wider understanding of the drivers and context, student and sector needs, and allows re-framing of practice within a curriculum framework (Manouchehri, 2002);

b. recognition of the role played by values in driving judgement and action and decision-making as a professional; this may involve resolving conflicts between personal, professional, organisational and societal values;

c. a need to engage with wider scholarship and theories on practice in particular on issues of teaching and learning within the subject field and at the appropriate level of learning.

The critical professional module requires participants to engage critically with a scholarly inquiry into an issue or aspect of their practice and to consider implications. Output includes draft articles, critical papers and an annotated bibliography. The notion of critical reflection which underpins the module is informed by Larrivee's model of reflection (2008) and Brookfield (1995).

To summarise: at postgraduate diploma stage, modules develop research methodology and understanding based on educational and qualitative and interpretive approaches to research, which allow the development of skills and understanding of methods, enabling research into the student experience and the student 'voice' and supporting participants in gaining insight into those aspects of their practice they wish to develop. An action research module encourages critical perspectives on action research because of its ongoing 'contested' nature, as well as the design of action research interventions which participants can then implement and pursue as research. Within this group of modules there is a module about writing and academic dissemination media. This develops communication confidence and educational literacy so that practitioners can not only develop their practice through research and critical reflection, but also disseminate it through appropriate, relevant journals and media, making their learning part of the wider professional knowledge base. Through these structured spaces we feel we establish strong foundations for practitioners to engage in development that reflects the models of Healey and Jackson (2004) and Yorke (2000).

The final masters project is designed to allow practitioners to pursue an applied practitioner research project and to develop skills and knowledge through acting as researcher-practitioners. The project uses workshops and action learning sets to ensure that participants are able to use the community to share, disseminate and construct learning applied to problems and issues. Because practitioners on the programme are largely in full-time employment, the module frames the process around the research supporting progress and completions and the achievement of deadlines within very busy lives. The project also acts as an opportunity to pilot methodology and methods as preparation for transfer into a doctoral stage within the progression route.

Through the process of periodic course review, we have rationalised diverse programmes and certificates to create a 'ladders and bridges' model of professional learning and education studies. This enables both progression and crossover. It adopts a practitioner focus, structuring a progression route from continuing professional development awards to the MEd and professional doctorate (EdD). Parallel to this, it has a subject route focusing on pure education research, via an MA in educational research and on to PhD. The recent addition of a further masters in education route incorporating national curriculum subjects means that we are increasingly focusing on professional practitioner development across several sectors. This is why for me the MEd framework is exciting: it provides a route to professional scholarship and professional mastery (see Figure 4.1).

The final stage of the framework takes the form of a professional doctorate providing an equivalent practitioner doctoral route to complement the existing PhD in education. The aim in designing this was to target the 'scholarly professional in education' (Doncaster and Thorne, 2000) rather than to train the professional researcher in education as would be the goal of a PhD. Consequently, the professional doctorate provides a practitioner-focused route to doctoral study, based around ideas of community and knowledge construction for practitioners, extending the idea of the professional practitioner enshrined within the MEd. The MEd forms stage one of a two-tier professional doctorate programme. Stage two of the professional doctorate is supported using facilitated classes for each cohort, providing a structure for the research process and the writing of the thesis. In this way we meet research regulations and provide appropriate support whilst ensuring a practitioner-applied and reflexive focus to the award. Applying models of knowledge (Scott *et al.*, 2004), the professional doctorate assumes that at the doctoral level of study for a professional field, in this case as a professional educator, the practitioner is able to use research not only to enhance practice, but to develop new knowledge and to contribute to the codified knowledge base for the profession.

Figure 4.1 The Masters in Education (MEd) framework

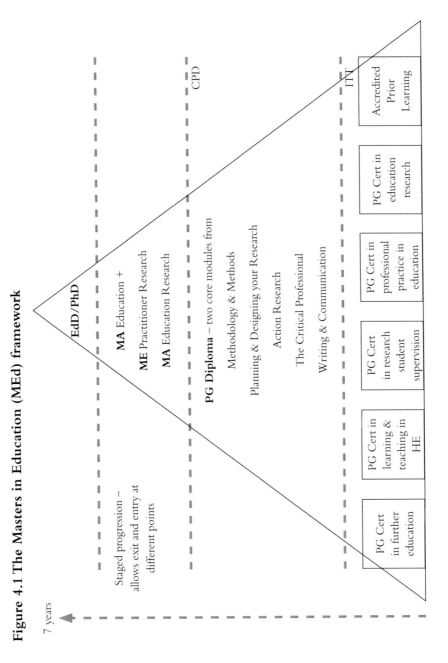

Discussion

A particular benefit for the programme has been its relocation within a wider partnership framework. The course team is responsible for a postgraduate certificate in further education delivered in several regional colleges, and the route into the MEd from the postgraduate certificate in further education has stimulated significant growth in student numbers. Furthermore, interest in the professional doctorate from practitioners on the MEd and in the region has been high. The increase in numbers on the award indicates that the MEd has gained status through the partnership further education route and shows the potential for professional learning from this award to influence organisational learning: three completions in 2008, four in 2009, eight in 2010, over 20 in 2011 and over 30 in 2012. Whilst this growth may not continue in the current climate and funding environment for post-compulsory and higher education, I believe it is evidence that the philosophy of the MEd as an enabling continuing professional development structure has been accepted.

The EdD is part of a tradition of professionally-orientated doctorates which recognise the contribution and value of original practitioner knowledge formulated in the workplace and as a result of practice-oriented, applied research (Fell, Flint and Haines, 2011). It offers a route for higher education and post-compulsory lecturers to develop beyond the scholarly practice of the MEd, generating original knowledge that is relevant to practice and is research-led. The professional doctorate provides a structure and space for the professional educational practitioner to complete a journey, attaining a central position within the educational community and contributing new knowledge to their community of practice on the basis of inquiry and original practitioner research. In designing this stage of the award we have adopted a theoretically informed view of professional knowledge, drawing on Scott *et al.*'s (2004) discussion of 'modes of knowledge'. For us, the design of the professional doctorate and its feeder programme is about developing the capacity of the professional educator to create critical knowledge, which is complex, influenced, generated and enacted in and around research into practice.

In the professional doctorate there are issues such as challenges to the individual in conceptualising the knowledge base, challenges founded in practitioner research and ethics, organisational and implementation challenges, and challenges of identity. It is widely acknowledged that part-time doctoral students struggle to sustain engagement and balance while pursuing a PhD route to doctoral status (Wellington and Sykes, 2006; Watts 2008) because of isolation and limitations in the way that the PhD process is structured around an individual route. The professional doctorate makes use of modules and a cohort approach to ensure that peer support and discussion is facilitated, and that research and procedural requirements are framed through the programme structure. In this way community support is provided, structures are generated to frame discourse within the process, and space is created for skills to develop and confidence and reflexivity to be engaged with. Additionally, two modules on organisational impact and change, delivered as part of stage two, draw on ideas about organisational learning and change, suggesting that the researcher-practitioner on the course should engage with this as part of a professional responsibility to develop practice. This concept is implicit in the notion of academic leadership enshrined in the UK professional standards framework at descriptor three. The professional should, upon attaining proficiency and membership in the core of the community, become a leader and influencer of change.

The structure of the doctorate has a positive impact on ensuring steady progress and timely completion (Wellington and Sykes, 2006; Drake with Heath, 2011), and should strengthen the impact of the professional doctorate for both individual and organisation. Certainly, in our view, it has already created a community that is becoming a focus for leading dissemination and enhancement of practice. As the process of developing the scholarly practitioner is framed within a community of practice approach, it enables us to offer regular seminars with invited external speakers and to run conferences on sharing practice and poster events that support professional learning.

The courses and awards we have designed assume academics have to be as scholarly about their teaching and learning practice as they are in researching their own subjects. This responds to models of professional education that are promulgated in the higher education sector in particular. Through the formal learning situations of the MEd, we have tried to build in processes, and supported progression and a safe learning environment. We achieved this by concentrating the learning around the practice setting through the work-based focus of assignments and through a social discursive process in sessions, ensuring that exploration of practice is informed and supported by scholarship.

The MEd programme provides formal learning for professionals that can enhance continuing professional development, have an impact on institutions, support disciplinary approaches and interdisciplinary learning, and integrate leadership and academic development. Our model begins with an ideal, a picture of identity within which a key aim is to support the professional higher education practitioner in building an identity around teaching and learning. The focus for this is the scholarly practitioner. This is someone who has both the subject expertise and the specialist knowledge that is the hallmark of post-compulsory education. It is someone who also has specific understanding and knowledge of core concepts in relation to teaching, learning and assessment. The practitioner's subject knowledge may be evident in postgraduate qualification or in vocational or professional expertise in a field of employment that the specialist lecturer can bring into the curriculum, benefiting the students. The challenge is that within further and higher education sectors, where primacy is given to subject specialist knowledge, the practitioner often lacks the necessary pedagogic literacy, concepts and skills. Our experience suggests these can be acquired through courses taking the professional from attaining initial professional competency to continuing professional development, and ultimately, leadership and development of educational practice for the subject.

We have found that the postgraduate certificate gives new members of staff confidence and a theoretical framework to inform interventions in teaching delivery and critical reflection and evaluation of impact. This is illustrated in the quotes from participants:

> *The sessions/topics you collectively provided on reflective practices, lesson planning, group work, have all contributed very positively to my own teaching (and hopefully are being well received by my students!) I am also really keen on my pedagogic research on postgraduate learning approaches, and again, your enthusiasm on the postgraduate certificate programmes have been a huge motivation for me to pursue these interests further.* (Participant A)

> *I was really taken aback at how the overt and subtle learning opportunities offered over the teaching toolkit module and postgraduate certificate have been so incredibly powerful in terms of my knowledge base, teaching strategies and my ability to truly engage with students in a dynamic and meaningful manner.* (Participant B)

I've very much enjoyed doing the postgraduate certificate, the sessions were all particularly helpful in my day-to-day experience of teaching and learning sessions and it was a particularly good cohort and 'learning together' is now a central part of my philosophy of teaching. I also find I feel a lot more relaxed and comfortable in my role and am actually enjoying it much more. I'm now registered on modules towards the MEd target award, hopefully to complete in two years. (Participant C)

The MEd stage provides hands-on opportunities to engage in genuine formal research which can then be developed beyond the course, through discipline networks or at conferences, resulting in papers and leading to change – occasionally far-reaching, organisational change. Impact may be located initially within the team, local community or module, but our experience suggests the formal engagement in scholarship can result in more deliberate inquiry and professional practitioner research. This is something participants have clearly voiced in their comments:

I've really enjoyed it and I feel like I've really developed as a practitioner as well as an academic. (Participant D)

The opportunity to research and write on professional development within higher education is rarely available. However such a chance was offered in seeking to gain the award of Master of Education. … The findings had a direct impact upon my own professional development, in designing curriculum content and the implementation of increased variety in teaching, learning and assessment strategies. A clearer recognition of the student experience and the implications of contemporary society informed not only what I did, but how I did it. I feel fortunate to have achieved such insight into a 'real world' understanding of education as it is lived by those who invest in it daily. (Participant E)

It has been hard, but a pleasure. (Participant F)

I have found it really useful doing this and feel I am now getting to grips with not only the literature relevant to my project, but also methodology and paradigms. … Anyway, I feel like I am really getting to grips with it after this exercise. (Participant G)

Finally, the professional doctorate produces even more fundamental change, as these participant comments indicate:

> *The advantages for me are self-growth as an academic and individual, peer-relationships and support. A key advantage is also that the professional doctorate has a time frame and therefore completion date is set rather than taking a number of years writing a thesis. Finally, the professional doctorate can be adapted for both internal and external communities of practice which is important in today's ever-changing marketplace and academic environments.* (Participant H)

> *I find that the whole process changes you as a person and your perceptions in your everyday working life. The professional knowledge you gain is not only through the research but more importantly how you come to view your own working practices.* (Participant J)

> *Once you start to engage with professional knowledge your viewpoints change.* (Participant K)

Professional learning supported through courses can increase satisfaction and interest in the teaching role and develop confidence to change practice. This may be particularly important for those feeling pressured in the current economic climate, but is essential for ongoing purposive reflection and professional development of practice. We suggest our courses can be used as a model for others to transform practice and professional identities and understanding, and ultimately have an impact upon the nature and success of the educational process.

CHAPTER FIVE

Bringing about the shift from knowledge acquisition to critical thinking in higher education students

Christine Hough

Introduction

This chapter is a discussion of one higher education teacher's experiences of developing teaching strategies on a new degree programme, and how these have evolved in response to students' learning and employability needs. The case study describes how a module has responded to the recognition that early years students on a degree lacked critical thinking skills. It draws on experiences of teaching third-year students on the year-long core module for a recently validated bachelor of arts honours (BA Hons) degree programme, Children, Schools and Families. Whilst the case study describes in detail the teaching strategy developed to enhance these skills, the impetus for this change was recognition that these early years students lacked essential professional skills, in particular critical thinking. The lack of these skills, it is argued, prevented students from being able to evaluate policy and relate this to their practice settings. Whilst studying successfully in a higher education setting, their individual professional development was felt to be impaired by this inability to evaluate policy and take account of the wider context. The case study reflects an outside–in direction as represented in our model in the way it responds to policy and knowledge required by professional bodies and creates a formal learning space to support this response.

The module in question is entitled 'Learning from Work', and the case study relates the way that the perception of the rationale for teaching the course content has evolved around it. Over the last two years this rationale has shifted from an initial aim of teaching students 'about' policy and practice into one that intends to lead, or guide, students to adopting a more critical stance towards engagement with course content. This change in rationale, or the ethos of teaching approach, has taken place through the development of teaching and learning activities closely structured around the elements of critical thinking. They comprise tasks that simulate, as closely as is possible, a range of different scenarios/sets of circumstances that students are likely to encounter in the workplace.

Target audience – making students critical

These teaching approaches have evolved in order to facilitate students' understanding of the broader contexts of the key issues that are at the heart of the course content, and comprise a blend of methods, including interactive tasks designed to develop the students' capacity to take on alternative perspectives in their own writing and thinking. The tasks encourage them to appraise critically the standard of their own, and others', professional practice through the prism of government and research documentation, serious case reviews, commissioned reports and Ofsted inspection reports. Through their engagement with practice-based learning activities, such as group discussion, report writing and observing and recording different types of care provision, students are encouraged to understand how to distinguish between 'hard' evidence and mere description. This aspect of their learning reflects the extent to which they have acquired and understood the skills of evaluation and making judgements about what they read and see. Once they are able to do this, they can reflect critically on provision in their own settings and begin to identify the strengths and areas for improvement. These skills are at the heart of effective self-evaluation, which in turn provides the basis for constructing a strategic development/improvement plan – a key function of the role of senior management and leadership. This chapter can be viewed as a case study of the types of teaching strategies that support the development of students' advanced workplace skills, designed to encourage them to foster a critically professional stance in their learning and engagement with policy and practice.

The enabling structure – using course content to develop criticality

I use the example of one module in particular to illustrate this – the Learning from Work module. The learning outcomes for the module provide the basis of my planning for all teaching and learning activities, as they are the part of the framework on which students are assessed. These are worth mentioning here because they define the requirements for critical thinking:

1. Identify and critically analyse the principles and practice that underpin effective provision in your chosen setting, relating to one or more policy frameworks of central significance for the operational practice of your chosen setting.
2. Demonstrate an evidence-based understanding of service user participation and the welfare requirements for children and young people in a specific service context or setting.
3. Demonstrate an in-depth knowledge of the roles and responsibilities of professionals within the education and/or social care sectors.
4. Demonstrate a critically informed understanding of organisational culture and the influential potential of the practitioner as an agent for change.

These learning outcomes reflect the importance of the skills of critical analysis and evaluation and the need to understand the complexities of working in welfare, care or educational settings, with regard to the students' own and others' professional roles. The majority of students were studying on this year-long core module work as full-time or part-time practitioners, in a range of child-care and educational settings, such as early years nurseries, pupil referral units, children's centres and schools. However, several will only have experienced work settings on the placements they completed in the first and second year of the course. There are two distinct cohorts of students; those who have reached their third year of study after gaining a foundation degree at a local partner college, and those who are the (first) cohort of third-year undergraduates studying the honours degree programme from its year of inception in 2010.

Much of what students learn on the Learning from Work module can be classified as professional development, rather than purely acquisition of new knowledge. I have to be realistic, as many students on the course have very patchy knowledge and understanding of the professional landscape of the children and young people's workforce. Therefore, much of what I teach is designed to encourage students to reflect, question and critically analyse professional practice across settings and in the documents we analyse. When I first began teaching the module, I assumed that students would automatically understand what a 'policy' is; it was only when I conducted a workshop on assignment-building that I realised that students had enormous difficulty in identifying where and how their own professional practice was shaped by changes to policy. These were significant reports and events such as the Laming Inquiry (Department of Health and Home Office, 2003), the Every Child Matters (ECM) initiatives (Department for Education, 2003) and the amendments to the Children Act (2004). For example, a student recently asked me if she could use the policy of inclusion as the focus for her assignment, saying 'Or do I need to use a "political policy"?' This is typical of the gaps in many students' knowledge and understanding about policy and reforms that have shaped the structure of their own workforce. Therefore, much of what they are learning and starting to understand from this module provides them with ideas and initiatives which they can take back to their own work setting to help improve the quality of provision.

This has been true of the workshops we have had regarding leadership and management and the Common Core of Skills and Knowledge (CCSK) (Department for Education and Skills (2005) and CWDC (2010)). After two taught sessions, in which students produced a case study on a child who had presented with mental health problems, one student produced a summary of the six key areas of the CCSK and asked her work manager if she could circulate these to all practitioners in the setting, including the part-time staff and volunteers. The manager had never heard of this document, despite its significance as a means of inducting professionals into the key areas of knowledge and skills that help and support professionals working with children and young people.

Through their degree students learn about the key policies and guidance for practice that have contributed to the major reforms to the children and young people's workforce over recent years. What the students then discover is that many of the managers and practitioners in their own settings have never heard of these developments and do not incorporate them into their own professional practice. On one hand, this means that sometimes the students themselves are able to introduce elements of professional development to their settings, with the support of their managers. On the other hand, students may experience antagonism towards their own input, when managers may feel under threat from a 'junior' practitioner who is more knowledgeable about policy and practice than they are. This is a distinctive characteristic of the degree programme and this particular module; that it contributes both to students' learning and to their ongoing professional development.

More broadly, whilst practitioners in early years settings are eligible to take the training for the Early Years Professional Status (EYPS) award if they are graduates, it is not a prerequisite to have a cognate or relevant degree, so practitioners could be graduates in geography, music or any other subject discipline unrelated to children, schools and families. This highlights an area in which the award of professional status may not actually be contributing to the professional development of practice in work settings, but rather focusing on the singular role of the senior practitioner who completes the course.

Discussion

During the first year of teaching this core content, I came to realise that an important facet was absent in students' discussions and written tasks. They could speak about their professional practice eloquently, but they used none of the terminology and vocabulary that I would have expected from a practitioner working in a children and young people's setting. I realised early on that I needed to structure a framework within which students could interpret their work experience in terms of relevant policies and documentation, but with a critical edge. This critical edge would show the extent to which they regarded central policies as realistic to their own settings, or how effectively they could evaluate the quality of the provision. They lacked a context or frame of reference for this because many of them were not familiar with the significance of aspects of reflective practice such as self-evaluation, the nature of the roles of leadership and management and the role of strategic development in planning.

The importance of context is not to be underestimated. Understanding the context of a situation will enable professionals to better understand/ make sense of what they see and read. Students who have critical thinking skills will better understand the context within which they work, or do their placement, and so will be able to analyse and evaluate the practice and policies more sharply (Hughes, 2000). Paulson (2011) makes the case clearly, explaining that 'critical thinking occurs at the highest level when thinkers must deal with an ill-structured problem that that does not have a single correct answer' (p. 400), showing the need to provide a real context using a reality-based project. These insights may help to explain why students are often unwilling to share their summarised accounts or short reports, saying that 'I'm probably wrong'. They have not yet reached the higher level of critical thinking where they can address the 'ill-structured problem' of answering a complex, yet very open task. This requires distilling evidence from an article or summarising recorded observations to which there is no 'right' or 'wrong' answer.

Finn (2011) adds to this analysis:

> *Critical thinking is the ability and willingness to assess claims and make objective judgements on the basis of well-supported reasons and evidence rather than emotion or anecdote. They realise that criticising an argument is not the same as criticising the person making it ... is not merely negative thinking. It includes the ability to be creative and constructive... .* (Finn, 2011: 70)

The most significant areas of weakness in students' levels of understanding, their capacities to be evaluative and creative, can be usefully analysed in terms of Bloom's original taxonomy and the revised taxonomy. This helps to identify more precisely the areas in which students struggle to achieve the 'higher order' aspects of thinking critically.

In Figure 5.1, the left-hand side (a) shows the structure of Bloom's original taxonomy, with the most basic level of classification of thinking at the bottom of the pyramid, in the form of 'knowledge'. The highest classification of thinking is in the top tier and is called 'evaluation'. The revised taxonomy, on the right-hand side (b), shows how these terms have been re-defined as part of the major update of the original taxonomy, designed to 'add relevance for twenty-first-century students and teachers' (Forehand, 2001: 2), where the highest classification of thinking has been re-defined as 'creating'. The most relevant aspect of the revised taxonomy for this discussion is that the original one-dimensional taxonomy has now been revised into a two-dimensional model. The first of these two dimensions, the cognitive dimension of knowledge, is shown in Figure 5.1b. From the diagram I can identify that the root cause of students' difficulties with being creative and evaluative are due to the fact that they have scant understanding of course concepts and therefore cannot readily remember them; this also makes it difficult for them to go on to analyse and apply these concepts to the tasks they work on in their taught sessions. In the revised taxonomy, the original category of knowledge/comprehension (see Figure 5.1a) has changed to understanding, which helps to explain more fully the context of students' poor basic knowledge.

For the purposes of my own teaching, the change in terminology suggests a greater imperative to the skills concerned. I am striving to facilitate students in actually doing, or performing, the skills and this is

Figure 5.1 Diagram showing (a) Bloom's original taxonomy and (b) the revised taxonomy

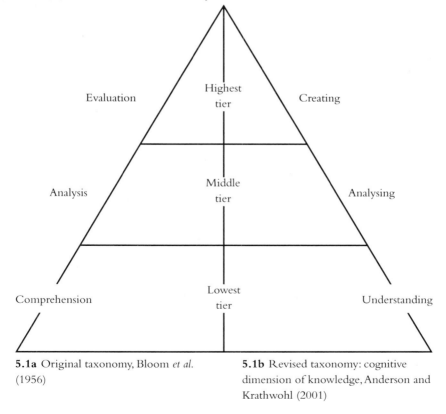

5.1a Original taxonomy, Bloom *et al.* (1956)

5.1b Revised taxonomy: cognitive dimension of knowledge, Anderson and Krathwohl (2001)

what they are reluctant to do, because their underlying knowledge is poor. In the revised version of the knowledge dimension of Bloom's taxonomy, the highest level of knowledge involves 'meta-cognition', which relates closely to the skills of critical thinking. Many of the students with significant work-based experience often find it difficult to understand the meaning of concepts and theory and how they apply to their own professional practice. This higher level of 'knowledge' is what I am striving to help them reach, through the development of their critical thinking skills. Looking back on my observations of and reflections on these taught sessions with year three students, I can see that some of the areas of knowledge, and its application, with which they struggle the most are remembering new knowledge acquired in previous sessions; being able to take an overview of a document or article and understand its purpose; and relating research content, theory or an area of policy to their own professional experience. These aspects are identified in the two reflections I have taken from my lecture notes during October–November 2012.

Reflection 1:

With regard to the final task, we got as far as the first question: what is the purpose of the report? A few could hazard a short phrase – they don't seem to be able to carry over what they learned from the previous week …

Reflection 2:

Completing the handout of life-chance measures was mostly done best (as far as I could see) by those students who work full time. This is to be expected as they have so much more work-based experience. The second group had better, more relevant and practical suggestions for indicators that would be of value to them. I think because this group is smaller, it is easier for them as a group to exchange their personal experiences. The exchange of suggestions was valuable and useful, because some of them were very down to earth and practical and so provided insights into certain aspects of a child's home background/context in which other students have very little experience.

In Reflection 1, aspects of the revised taxonomy that are significant in the challenges presented to the students include those of applying and evaluating (see Figure 5.1b). However, I think that the students' difficulty in remembering work done in previous sessions is also connected to their lack of understanding of the concepts they are introduced to, relating to the revised knowledge dimension of understanding, shown in the lower tier of Figure 5.1b. In Reflection 2, those students with extensive work-based experience are beginning to apply what they are learning to situations they encounter in their work. There is evidence of them making interesting critical analyses of the life-chance measures mentioned, because they are seeing how these relate to real-life examples in their work place.

From the above diagrams and discussions, I can identify the following categories from the revised taxonomy as being the most significant to the development of students' critical thinking and advanced learning skills: cognitive processes that are defined as creating, evaluating, applying and analysing; whilst the knowledge dimension is defined as metacognition. In other words, this level of knowledge is connected to the extent to which a student can think about their own thinking in order to recognise what they need to do to improve how they think.

Examples of teaching strategies

In this section I include two or three examples of how I incorporated the above elements of critical thinking skills and professionalisation into structured tasks, and analyse the outcomes in terms of students' knowledge and understanding and the extent to which they do, or do not, demonstrate aspects of critical thinking skills.

Ennis (2011) defines critical thinking as reasonable and reflective thinking that is focused on deciding what to believe or do. This can be described as a reasonable and authentic process that involves high standards concerning accuracy, relevance and depth. From my recent experiences of teaching on this degree programme, it is precisely these latter actions that many year three students are unable to carry out with regard to interactive tasks. They are always nervous about completing any written tasks in lectures. From discussions with students, I think this nervousness in getting started with any written task stems from their own very basic or scant knowledge of the relevant contemporary issues, concepts and policies. Whilst many students have a great deal of workplace experience, they have very little experience of evaluating aspects of the provision in their work setting within any sort of framework such as the Every Child Matters policies, or Ofsted's framework of evaluation for inspections. Through the structured teaching strategies, my aim is that students will produce outcomes such as reports and critical analyses, to encourage them to be evaluative and to apply what they are learning to their analyses of examples of practice and provision.

In the two examples that follow, I present the interactive tasks I have designed to facilitate the development of students' critical thinking skills, and my reflections on outcomes in which students have successfully demonstrated in their responses. I have focused mainly on the following aspects of critical thinking, as I have interpreted them:

- to develop the skills of evaluation and making judgements about what they read and see;
- to reflect critically on provision, either in their own settings or from written/visual evidence, and begin to identify the strengths and areas for improvement;
- to interpret their work experience in terms of the relevant policies and documentation, but with a critical edge.

Example 1: Susan's Story (October 2012)
Outline of task

Students worked with recorded observations they had made in response to watching a video clip, entitled 'Susan's Story', early on in the semester. In this video, a little girl narrates the circumstances of her life at home and at school. She is highly vulnerable and her stories about her parents'/ carers' behavior at home gave clear indications of extreme neglect of both her physical and emotional health.

Students shared their recorded observations amongst the group and were asked to agree on a list of five to six items of evidence that they considered to be the most significant, in terms of the child's well-being. They were to arrive at this consensus after discussing their observations in terms of the relevant formal terms, phrases and vocabulary we had recently analysed within the literature of government policies and guidance documents. They then had to draw up an action plan of recommended interventions to support Susan and her family. These were focusing on the following aspects of Susan's well-being: her achievement; relevant aspects of safeguarding evident in her school setting; and relevant examples of the five outcomes included in the Every Child Matters policies (stay safe, stay healthy, enjoy and achieve, make a positive contribution, and make an economic contribution). The structure and wording of the report had to be accessible to a multi-agency team of professionals from across the welfare agencies such as social work, health, education and social services. Key words included: vulnerable; intervention; health; hygiene; safeguarding; at risk.

I prepared a range of resources to support the activity in class. These included a video and PowerPoint slide to support the task and role-play cards, as I indicate below:

- The video was drawn from a series of structured videos located on the Department of Education's website under the overarching title of 'Childhood Neglect'.
- I created a PowerPoint slide with pictures to stimulate ideas and clues to the relevant aspects of Susan's health and well-being.
- I provided printed labels with fictitious names of local authority teams on them. Students selected these at random and these pre-determined the teams they worked in (four people maximum). For example:
  ○ Multi-agency team, NHS primary care trust
  ○ Multi-agency team, youth offending team and social services
  ○ Multi-agency team, children's services

Example of work completed for Susan's Story – analysis and report. Group A:

Susan's story highlights a number of issues which could be detrimental to her development. In order to address these issues, it would be good practice for the teacher to contact the school's parent liaison officer (PLO) and ask them to contact social services, as the family may already be known to them. (This would be a precautionary measure.) The PLO may also contact the school nurse and check whether or not Susan has been signed up to the local GP practice.

It would be important for the teacher, school nurse and the PLO to have a meeting with the parents to discuss what Susan has disclosed to her teacher in order to guide them in terms of accessing services such as Sure Start for support in setting a routine for Susan and her brother. This meeting would also be beneficial in order to explain the importance of getting Susan to the dentist and the GP when needed, as well as the implications of poor personal hygiene and diet in reference to Susan's well-being. Hopefully, the parents will take this advice and support on board in order to improve Susan's well-being.

Recommended review: 2/3 weeks.

Whilst this report reads well from the perspective of its formal vocabulary and its accessibility to different welfare agency team professionals, there is no evidence of links with or reference to any of the five Every Child Matters outcomes, or the specific aspects of safeguarding, as we had analysed them during the taught sessions. We had read and discussed sections from a government document on safeguarding and, as part of an independent written task I set them, students had also applied these to their own settings and professional experiences. Despite this, many of them could not identify and apply these issues to the case study of Susan's story.

My reflections (as recorded in my lecture notes at the time)

1. Mixing students up by using team labels/titles worked very well, because the year three honours degree undergraduates ended up working with the year three foundation degree students, the latter having considerably more workplace experience on which to draw and to share.

2. There were robust, focused debates going on amongst the groups, and they asked plenty of questions to clarify their understanding of the task as they came closer to the moment of writing the report. They found two things difficult when identifying points and linking them into their report: firstly, any of the five ECM outcomes and, secondly, aspects from the safeguarding document we had analysed and discussed previously.

3. I asked them to post these reports on the relevant discussion thread on the virtual learning environment, (VLE). Only five teams out of about 12 did so – very disappointing.

These recorded reflections on the outcomes of the session are positive in terms of the students' responses to collaborating and how a team of multi-agency professionals would be expected to work. However, something they all found challenging was addressing the moment when they had to put their agreed analyses, ideas and recommendations into a formal, final report. They showed almost as much anxiety about this as if

106

they were about to commence a formal assessment or examination. This was even more apparent by the disappointing outcome of only five out of 12 groups actually completing and posting their report on the VLE.

Group A, who collaborated on the above report, were not able to assess and summarise the video clip using 'well-supported reasons and evidence rather than emotion or anecdote' (Finn, 2011: 2). The entire report is well-constructed and written, but only in terms of the *drama* of the little girl's narrative or story; there is no application of course theory or concepts. This could be a reflection of how little the students remembered and understood from the previous sessions, which suggests that they had not fully understood the context of the formal documentation and concepts.

Example 2: Analysis of a serious case review and an Ofsted report (February 2013)

Outline of task

Students analysed two documents:

- A serious case review (Plymouth Safeguarding Board, 2010) of the events in an early years setting in which a practitioner took pornographic photographs of children aged below five years. The practitioner then sent the photographs to her boyfriend who circulated them across a known pedophile ring in the UK. These events came to light because the setting was identified, in one of the photographs, by its logo on the practitioner's shirt, which she accidentally included when taking the photograph.
- The Ofsted inspection report of the same early years setting, conducted in 2007.

Students were directed to read both documents, collaboratively, and identify evidence that linked directly to aspects of leadership and management and of safeguarding. Students worked individually on two tasks:

1. Write a critical evaluation of the issues raised that relate to leadership and management.
2. Write a critical evaluation of the issues raised that relate to safeguarding.

We had spent the two previous sessions analysing critically the separate aspects of leadership and management as they apply to a range of settings for the children and young people's workforce and with regard to the criteria included in Ofsted's inspection schedules. The work on safeguarding related to earlier taught sessions at the time of the first example, Susan's Story (October, 2012) and also to sessions only one or two weeks previously.

Examples of work completed for summary and evaluation of serious case review and Ofsted report
Student A

From the Ofsted report in 2007, as an early years practitioner, it is shocking that the nursery received a satisfactory judgment as opposed to inadequate. Management of this setting appeared poor as policies were incomplete or not in place. The report states that there were adequate systems in place for the recruitment of staff, however, there was no system in place for updating Criminal Records Bureau documentation ensuring that all staff remain suitable to work with children. Both these issues highlight serious concerns with regards to the competence of the management of the nursery, which later proved detrimental to the children in the setting. One of the main, and most important, roles of management within an early years setting is ensuring all children are safeguarded and protected.

Student B

Ofsted identified that there was no 'formalised system for ensuring that staff remain suitable to work with children'. This is a serious safeguarding issue as the Criminal Records Bureau checks are not kept up to date, which could mean that staff who were no longer suitable to work with children could be working within the setting and become a potential risk to the well-being of the children. Therefore this could highlight that the staff recruitment policy was not up to date or could not have existed, which puts children at serious risk within a childcare setting.

A good example of where safeguarding of staff and children took place was in that all staff had taken part in 'good induction procedures' and were aware of their 'roles and responsibilities'. This meant that all staff knew where relevant fire exits were within the building and knew their role within their given room.

In contrast to the first example, students worked on the task for this individually and on computers. They then posted their evaluations, during the taught session, directly onto a journal tool that I set up on the virtual learning environment. For me, the most striking evidence apparent in these two examples is the extent to which the students are making effective evaluations about what they have read. This is a big step forward in their progress from the outcomes discussed in the first example towards acquiring the higher order skills of critical thinking. I tried to set up the climate for being evaluative by suggesting students use phrases in their writing such as: 'the Ofsted report said … and I agree/disagree because…; or 'the management was inadequate because…'. In both of these examples, the students are writing evaluatively and beginning to be creative in the way they qualify their evaluations. For example, when student B writes: '… this could highlight that the staff recruitment policy was not up to date or could not have existed … which puts children at risk', she is showing that she has analysed the relevant evidence of the safeguarding provision, in terms of the absence of a formal system for Criminal Records Bureau checks, applied this to a consideration of what the potential (negative) outcomes of this could be and extrapolated, or inferred, the overall judgement that this could put children at serious risk. Student A also writes evaluatively about the evidence in the Ofsted report and links this to the effectiveness of management in the setting.

These two short summaries show evidence of students beginning to answer a complex, open question competently and also to make judgements that are based on 'well-supported reasons and evidence rather than emotion or anecdote' (Finn, 2011: 22). The second example shows an improvement in students' thinking and writing skills and provides some evidence of the higher order skills of critical thinking. Between the first and second examples, students completed another four months of learning, including eight or so taught sessions, and this may well be the reason for the improvements shown in their work.

In the first example, in common with others at the time, the student writes competently, but the content of the report is based on Susan's story, or the unfolding drama of her life as she tells it to the camera. There is no analysis of evidence within the framework of policy or practice, and the content is purely based on the emotion and anecdote referred to by Finn (2011: 22). In the second example we can see clear evidence of students analysing the documentation and their application of learned topics, such as leadership, management and safeguarding, to the documents. This shows that they have understood the context of what they have learned and, from this, been able to make objective judgements, or evaluations about the claims made in both the serious case review and the Ofsted report. Their skills in making these evaluations also reflect the higher level of their knowledge, as shown in Figure 5.1b of the cognitive dimension of knowledge in the revised taxonomy. They have progressed from not being able to remember or understand what they have learned, which was the case in the early stages of the module, to demonstrating the higher tiers of knowledge in the revised taxonomy: applying, analysing, evaluating and creating. Above, I discuss the creating tier of knowledge in the revised taxonomy where students are extrapolating or inferring their judgements about the serious case review and Ofsted report, both of which terms I consider to be closely related to the creative process.

CHAPTER SIX

Writing as professional development

Yvon Appleby

Introduction

This chapter is a more complex example within the terms of our model as it comprises several small case studies showing how writing groups have benefited individuals. Whilst the other case studies have operated within the top half of our model, structured by organisation-led opportunities and the wider context respectively, this example is focused on the lower half, the practitioner-led field of the model. In each case the practitioners have been supported to develop a learning community, based around writing, to fulfil their own professional needs. In Example 1, 'Writing ourselves', a group of educational developers and teacher trainers are motivated to exploit the learning space offered by dedicated allocation of time and the enabling structure for writing a book. The second example, 'Writing about writing', also practitioner-led, was developed in response to an identified individual professional need within the postgraduate diploma programme. Many further education teachers on the programme lack academic and professional writing skills to act with confidence in their professional roles and in scholarly activities. The structure of the programme develops different types of writing practice; for example, developing academic posters, peer editing, writing a professional or academic article and writing a critical reflection. The learning space in this example therefore is more discrete and focused on the individual. The final example, 'Writing with and for others', is also an example of developing learning space, in this case a writing residential for those working in higher education. The enabling structured residential provides the opportunity for individuals to focus on their own academic writing; to complete articles, finish chapters and in some cases to start new writing.

There are many myths and assumptions around being able to write well. Some imply a predisposition where some people are 'naturally' good writers whilst others suggest the significance of the learning environment and curriculum, for example learning grammar. Whatever the received wisdom about being able to write, a significant number of teachers we have worked with express a difficulty, or limitation, in being able to write well in their professional capacity. Many explain that they have not had the chance to focus on or develop writing confidence and skills, either in graduate-level study or during and after qualifying as a teacher. In their descriptions of earlier writing, the criteria for success are often understood purely as academic content, with little emphasis on structure, flow and accessibility. This chapter suggests that writing for professional purposes can be developed by using a combination of contextual and collaborative methods which take account of purpose and audience, supported through peer review and critical editing. Good writing is not an innate ability but is something that can be learned and developed through practice.

The examples in this chapter, some of which cross the boundary between the further and higher education sectors, challenge assumptions about who writes and who reads the textual material we use in our professional lives as educators. It questions how this writing is produced and employed for different purposes. In these examples we challenge several assumptions which relate to our professional identity and professional practices. Firstly, we question and disrupt assumptions of who the producers and consumers of professional knowledge are, or can be. Secondly, we question the assumption that initial professional qualification enables teachers to learn critical writing skills which are 'fit for purpose' and need no further development. Thirdly, we suggest that viewing writing mainly as a solitary, or task-based activity, misses important aspects of critical learning and professional development supported through collaboration, feedback and critical questioning. Although often seen as task-based, individual and relying on existing skills, we suggest that structured writing can enhance and support critical professional development for educators across different sectors and contexts.

Target audiences

The examples in this chapter are drawn from our work in teacher education and professional development programmes where our collaborative
approaches have enabled us to link existing strands of work developing
new ideas and practices. We have also developed critically as professionals
through these activities as we have taken on new ideas and approaches
requiring us to think and write 'outside the box', challenging our own
assumptions and existing practices. The first example questions the
relationship between the production and consumption of educational
knowledge. It describes how managers in an initial teacher training
partnership were supported to write a book about their experiences
and beliefs and the challenges they faced in their professional roles. This
book was designed to support the individual professional development
of the managers as well as producing a teaching tool for the trainee
teachers they worked with. The second example questions the often
invisible assumption that teachers who are post-qualified are adequate –
or at least good enough – in writing, needing no further development,
learning or practice. This example describes a module within the
postgraduate diploma in professional practice in education which
is offered to teachers in further education and has been specifically
designed to support critical professional development post-qualification
through writing and professional communication. The third example
questions the belief that writing has to be task-based and solitary. It
describes a short residential collaborative workshop for university staff
which focused on writing for publication.

Example 1: Learning spaces – Writing ourselves

The initial teacher training programme at the University of Central
Lancashire is a large and diverse partnership covering the north west of
England. As part of the programme, all students undertake a compulsory
action research module enabling them to reflect upon and change their
practice using research. A selection of the research reports are published
annually in a university-sponsored journal *Through the Looking Glass*,
now in its sixth year, which is sold to the partner colleges and to the
next intake of students. The success of the journal in supporting individual professional development, for an average of 25 students a year, by
becoming published authors, prompted questions of developing a similar

writing space for the professional development of the teacher educators themselves. Eleven tutors and managers from the partnership responded to an open invitation to join a collaborative writing project to produce a book about teaching and learning written by them. All 11 – six women and five men – taught across a range of subject areas from catering to accountancy and, whilst willing to share their knowledge and understanding verbally, most had reservations about their writing ability and in having anything to say that would be worth reading. These are common fears expressed by those who work in education but are not practised at academic or scholarly writing (Morss and Murray, 2001; Murray, 2002; Moore, 2003; Murray *et al.*, 2008). The collaborative process was structured using two facilitated collaborative writing days with additional and continual online support (a fuller account is available in Appleby, 2009). The first of the two writing days, held at the university, provided a space to talk and discuss what was important in terms of teaching and learning. Most of the group commented that they didn't have this type of space in their everyday work which was bounded by increased workloads and an institutional focus on recruitment and retention. Away from everyday practical concerns, debates were at times heated as people reconnected with their politics and passion about teaching. From the discussions each person decided upon a focus for their own piece as insights and concerns were shared and worked on in small groups where ideas were refined and refocused. It was agreed not to have a template or overall writing style, instead allowing individual voices to represent the breadth of experiences, insight and intuition across the partnership.

A second writing day allowed authors protected space to write, discuss and edit each other's work more closely, becoming peer editors and mentors as well as writers. After the two writing days drafts were worked on with the editors by email, providing more flexibility for fitting in with busy timetables. Some writers found this stage in the process straightforward and merely tidied up pieces. For others this stage was more difficult either in adapting to academic conventions, such as providing references, or in questioning the authenticity of their piece and its relevance to readers. The book, called *Looking Back and Moving Forward: Reflecting on Our Practice as Teacher Educators* (Appleby and Banks, 2009), represents the issues and passions of the authors collectively: these were issues and insights they wanted to own and write about for themselves and for others. The chapters cover a range of material including, for example: looking at the experiences of vocational tutors managing their own learning, passing on significant motivational texts to counter cynicism, using images in teaching, using action research, mentoring and engaging with feminist pedagogy.

Discussion of Example 1

Feedback on the process of working collaboratively for publication highlighted both what was positive and what was challenging for the writers. Some comments reported a discomfort in becoming novices in (collaborative) writing rather than the more certain identity of confident teacher. Such a shift required identity negotiation and management, something experienced at times as uncomfortable and unsettling. The process of putting thoughts on paper to structure and write a chapter was described as difficult, with some explaining that 'writing is hard'. It was perceived that writing was something that was done by academics in university rather than by those who taught in further education. This illustrates the power of the assumption implicit in the distinction between 'thinking and writing' in higher education and 'doing' in further education: the notion itself being challenged in the process of writing the book. Struggling with writing did, however, act as a reminder of the difficulties students face as they undertake a programme that is predominately text-based assessment. The benefits described by the authors were in providing a supported space to think, talk and then write about practice and pedagogy. Discussions during the writing days, often continued independently in other forums, enabling a reassessment and reassertion of what mattered as each person reconnected and critically re-examined their ideas. Some of the discussion focused on policy and large-scale issues such as current educational ideology and feminist pedagogy, whilst other discussions focused on contextualised teaching practices, exploring alternative assessment for tutors with poor literacy, or using symbols in teaching.

Working collaboratively does not automatically create a space for critical professional development; the role of the facilitator was significant in achieving this. As facilitator I was able to explore and encourage ideas to be extended and revised in professional dialogue (see Brookfield, 1995). A dialogical approach enabled voices to be heard, ones which more often transmit the educational theories or ideas of others rather than speak for themselves. One contributor to the book wrote that it was 'the first chance to stop and think about issues I have felt strongly about but had not previously written about'. Another described the process as a joy, as he valued the chance to talk with like-minded colleague, something that seldom happened in further education; it was therefore for this writer hugely stimulating if rather exposing.

The process of writing the book provided a structured space to support critical professional development for the authors where they became 'authorised and authoritative writers' by using their own practice knowledge, insight and intuition as well as sharing their beliefs, passions and uncertainties. This produces a sense of being there, of being 'real', which corresponds to Zukas and Malcom's (2007) ideas of professional development where real people relate to students as real people in the real world of teaching and learning. The 'realness' is significant, as Bathmaker and Avis (2007) argue, in understanding how further education lecturers' identities are formed in the context of their students' behaviours and expectations.

One of the central themes expressed in the writing was a commitment to authenticity; that is as authenticity of self and in the professional role of teacher. Notions of authenticity and teacher identity were visible threads in the discussions and the finished chapters of the book. This concept is explored by Kreber *et al.* (2009: 41) who suggest that authenticity is a key concept in teaching and involves being genuine, being self-aware, being self-defined and bringing oneself into interactions with students. The collaborative writing produced a book which will support the learning of others by providing space for teacher educators to articulate, share and write about what matters to them as authentic professionals.

The book representing the authors' collective knowledge supported their development as teachers and writers, as well as the professional development of the intended audience. It is not simply the knowledge itself that is significant but the collaborative process, which allows a richer and more diverse set of knowledges and pedagogies to be shared, showing a greater range of practices and dilemmas from the 'real' world of teaching. The content of the book shows that collaborative writing can support critical, relevant reflective practice for those engaged in the process. It provides a place for counter-narratives (Giroux *et al.*, 1996) to be developed and accessed more widely in different domains. Importantly, publishing those who are more often readers than authors is a transgressive act (hooks, 1994), which challenges the power and ownership of the written word, unsettling modes of production and consumption of knowledge.

Example 2: Enabling structures – Writing about writing

The second example discusses a module from the postgraduate diploma in professional practice in education, which is part of our postgraduate professional development pathway. The postgraduate diploma is the first stage of the masters route leading to the MEd, which can be both an exit award as well as the first stage of the professional doctorate. The pathway is designed to provide a graduated and developmental approach to postgraduate study that provides the opportunity to carry out research into individual practice. The module discussed here, called 'Professional Writing and Communication', was developed by three experienced tutors to support the academic and professional writing of those taking the postgraduate diploma who work mainly in in the post-compulsory sector in further education colleges, with private providers or in work-based or community education. Having run the programme for several years it became apparent that many of those who worked in the post-compulsory sector on our programme struggled with aspects of academic writing and of professional communication. This prevented them obtaining the grades they deserved as well as learning new skills as part of their professional development. The module was therefore a response to a perceived learning need that we reflected our curriculum and teaching was not supporting. This is not to suggest that those in the post-compulsory sector who work in further education have fewer writing skills than colleagues in higher education, but that their different working environment may not provide the same continuing professional development opportunities for self-development and practice. The lifelong learning sector is varied and, as such, individual institutional continuing professional development opportunities may vary considerably.

The Professional Writing and Communication module has a flexible method of delivery and is usually taught in three-hour sessions every fortnight after the majority of day classes have finished. The sessions use a facilitative and collaborative approach where professional and everyday uses of writing are discussed and deconstructed using the concepts of audience and purpose as a guide. Rather than seeing writing merely as a technical skill to be acquired, we encourage the students, professional educators themselves, to consider the different purpose that we use writing for in our professional roles. Examples discussed include:

to give or ask for information, to express an opinion, to make an argument, to provide feedback, to explain a process or technique, to provide encouragement or to express concern. This encourages our postgraduate diploma students to connect to the different types of writing they use every day in their professional roles and practices. We discuss the different audiences that we communicate with in writing as part of our job, where examples show the range of people, as well as purposes, we communicate with in writing. These include managers, colleagues, schools, health professionals, exam boards, other institutions, employers, union officials, parents and of course students. This shows concretely that writing as a part of professional communication is more than a technique that can simply be applied across these many and varied contexts, audiences and purposes.

Discussion of Example 2

The students, as educators, will be aware and may be part of the ongoing concerns and initiatives around student writing. For those working in higher education programmes in further education there is a particular emphasis on graduate writing, with some authors describing the media as reporting a 'literacy crisis' (Ganobcsik-Williams, 2004). Those working in student or academic support have expressed inadequate writing skills as acting to 'disable' students and preventing learning (Davies *et al.*, 2006). The concern with difficulties in students' writing prompted some institutions to develop curricula interventions and technical workshops to support embedded writing skills at an institutional level (Fallows and Steven, 2000; Cox and King, 2006). Others have emphasised the experiential and social aspects of writing, rather than the technical aspects (Davies, 2000). Whilst we follow the second strand of thinking about writing – that it is social, situated and contextual – our experience suggests that the first strand is pervasive at all levels and across sectors. The common assumption across education sectors is that not being able to write as an undergraduate (or at any level) is viewed as a lack or deficit, and that technical remedial actions can improve writing skills. Whilst providing technical knowledge is important, teaching it as a decontextualised skill is not enough to support a wider understanding of the way that our different writing connects to each other or informs decisions about what is appropriate for a specific purpose and audience. This is why we deconstruct the writing practices that our students use in their professional roles using the framework of purpose and audience, as this enables the situated and contextualised nature of the writing to become apparent. We do look at techniques such as signposting, topic sentences and using voice, but these are embedded within wider discussion, collaborative activities and self and peer editing processes. In this way learning about writing is supported through exploration, trial, error and critical reflection.

As a way of experiencing writing in a different – and in this case a visual – medium, each student prepares and presents an academic poster on an aspect of their professional practice. To support critical thinking through writing each student also gives feedback to another participant identifying strengths and areas for them to develop. The posters as 'texts' are read for their clarity of purpose and ability to communicate with a specific targeted audience. The posters have covered topics such as employability skills, transition from further to higher education and notions of citizenship. Peer feedback on the posters questioned readability and suggested making language more accessible; having less text, which demonstrated knowledge but also confused the reader; and suggested visual signposting to give the reader structural reading cues. Although experienced as challenging, several of the teachers have implemented posters for learning and assessment within their own programmes, sharing their new knowledge with their students and colleagues. The creation of the posters, whilst requiring new technical knowledge, was valued by the students for exploring new ways of distilling writing, communicating information and sharing ideas. Some of the posters were presented at a university postgraduate conference on sharing practice, allowing practice knowledge to be articulated and shared in an academic setting – an environment felt to be outside the experience of those working in the post-compulsory and further education sector.

In additon, students prepare a sustained piece of writing which is informed by an issue or an aspect of their professional role. The 3,500-word piece is written for a target audience of other practitioners or professionals from the students' subject area, sector or role. It is intended to enable the student to develop a professional voice through writing and is, therefore, rigorous, scholarly and well-informed rather than academically hidebound, using an essay format for an academic audience. This more 'academic lite' professional writing approach is found to be challenging by the students as most want to reproduce a way of writing they have learned previously in their study but which, unlike this task, rarely required them to discuss their professional roles, knowledges and insights.

As part of the approach each student was given a writing buddy who reads and comments on the writing as it develops in terms of its intended purpose and from their perspective as the audience. This process posed several challenges for the students and the tutors. The first was a logistical issue as one student was out of the country for several weeks and another changed jobs, in both cases creating considerable time lag between the writing and editing stage. However, there have also been examples of practical ingenuity, such as developing a drop-box system to allow easy access between writing and editing. This was particularly valued by two students who accepted the challenge to write a piece jointly.

The second challenge was identified as knowing how to read and comment on a peer's work, as this had not been experienced before. There were dilemmas in knowing how to be critical without being negative and how to make suggestions without causing offence. At the beginning of the process, feedback was at the level of correcting typographical mistakes or in textual detail such as suggesting a new paragraph. As the process developed, supported by group discussion and looking at examples, the level of feedback generally became more critical and analytical rather than technical or descriptive. One or two of the group, who worked in the community, even though they felt they had developed their writing feedback, still expressed a discomfort and concern about not wanting to hurt their writing buddy's feelings. This prompted valuable discussion about the different contexts of the group's professional roles and the way that cultural, historical and social differences were experienced and negotiated in their different everyday professional writing practices. As a result of this writing task some postgraduate diploma students felt that they read practitioner writing in a different and more critical way, with several suggesting that they might contribute to a practitioner or professional journal in the future. This echoes the teacher educators above, who, in writing a book, unsettled boundaries between those who produced and those who consumed written knowledge about their practice. The postgraduate diploma students crossed a similar boundary seeing themselves as potential if not current contributors to practice-based professional journals and newsletters.

The final task in the Professional Writing and Communication module is a reflection of what has been gained and how any new skills, knowledge or insight can relate to their professional practice. Asked for reflections to include in this book, one student wrote:

> *It has enabled me to compose documents with a clearer understanding of the reader. I have been encouraged to develop my writing style to reflect what I want to say and to whom, in the most appropriate language/style/format. An understanding of how to use something as a simple as a poster to present information in a quick and striking way will be something I strive to use more when disseminating information to both students and peers. I also realised that with a bit more effort, I may indeed be capable of producing work of a high enough standard to gain recognition among my peers in professional publications, something that had not occurred to be before.*

Some of the reflections described students becoming more critical in their reading and the effect that this had upon their writing; others described taking more care and including new stages of editing in writing. Several wrote about becoming aware of how they wrote for the students they teach, ensuring that the purpose and writing was clear. Others commented that they would take more care in writing emails which, although considered by them to be informal communication, they acknowledged needed to be written clearly and effectively, with audience and purpose as significant factors.

Another postgraduate diploma student commented on the interactive and collaborative way of learning writing:

> *This particular way of studying meant that team-building skills were attained and greater involvement and participation. Group work was an integral part of the module which I felt was an excellent way of learning from my peers. Participation in this way of learning resulted in a new confidence that I never experienced before. I felt that because some of my peers were better acquainted with this type of writing I benefited in gaining new skills.*

This is clearly far removed from a simply technical skills approach to writing. As the postgraduate diploma student identifies in her writing, learning occurs through interaction and by sharing existing knowledge and insight. Through working with each other, barriers about getting it 'right' or 'wrong' were dismantled as we focused on relevance, clarity, authenticity, audience and purpose – all the things the postgraduate diploma students were knowledgeable in. Working collaboratively, even if producing a single authored work, as both Examples 1 and 2 above show, enables a richer and more diverse learning space to be developed. This will be illustrated in the next example which explores a short residential on writing for publication for staff working in a higher education institution.

Example 3: Learning spaces and enabling structures – Writing with and for others

This example discusses a short writing residential which focused on providing space and support for a small group of university staff to write for publication. Increasingly, academic members of staff are expected to produce scholarly work as part of their continuing professional development, outcomes which are often built into staff appraisal systems and promotion. At the same time, and existing alongside this expectation, increased workloads make it ever more difficult to find time to research and to write (Morss and Murray, 2001). To respond to some of these difficulties we organised a two-day writing residential for university staff working in the field of education and learning who had work that could be developed for publication. Seven colleagues responded to the invitation and started to plan a two-day gap in their diary to enable them to attend. Although the writing residential was free and was held near the university, several people said they were interested but were regrettably not able to free themselves of teaching or other commitments to be able to attend.

The writers were asked to bring abstracts, skeleton drafts or ideas with them to share and develop. The two days were structured around short workshops – which facilitated together with an experienced colleague from an adjoining university – individual writing, one-to-one support, peer-reviewing and editing. There were times when seven individuals sat with laptops busily writing followed by intense discussion and talk between pairs as they reviewed each other's work. The collaboration enabled sharing ideas, techniques and sources as each questioned the other about clarity and accessibility of the writing, the journal style, or format, and the intended audience. The group contained a mixture of novice writers as well as those who were more experienced but lacked time, space or motivation to complete writing already started. The mix was stimulating, as fresh eyes enabled new critical views to be expressed, whilst the voices of experience guided newer writers through some of the hurdles of reviewer comments and editing. The varied structure of individual writing and paired or group work changed focus and pace so interest and momentum was maintained throughout the two days. Most commented on how much they had written, or how the piece they were working on had developed in a short but concentrated time.

Discussion of Example 3

Uninterrupted time is a significant factor in what the participants expressed as their ability to write productively, as they were away from time-consuming daily routines and distractions. However, more than this, the approach acknowledges that writing is a social activity and as such it draws upon our culture, history and view of the world. The residential created a space of shared endeavour which, although not a programme, shares many of the findings that Morss and Murray (2001) found in their writing for publication programme which supported increased confidence and motivation in their university teacher participants. It created, albeit in a smaller timeframe, something similar to Clughen and Hardy's (2011) notion of a participatory or supportive writing culture. Although Clughen and Hardy's work was geared towards helping students develop their academic writing, it also took a social practice approach to literacy, questioning the simple skills approach in a similar way to our work. Clughen and Hardy, too, argue that writing spaces should support exploration of experiences not just techniques of writing. Our approach echoes their concern with creating an environment that affirms as well as challenges; spaces, they argue, should enable 'respectful, supportive and compassionate dialogues with each other, so it becomes meaningful and unique' (page xvi).

In the evening between the two days we asked the writers to reflect upon the day's activities and write what they had learned, valued or had struggled with. This was for some a difficult task and at least one writer felt it was a distraction to being able to progress with writing her article. However, the reflections shared the morning after showed that this process had enabled each writer individually to question their assumptions about how they worked, about what they wanted to communicate in their writing and who they were addressing it to. The writer who was initially least enthusiastic at producing a reflection agreed that looking at the process of writing was as important, if not

123

more important, than the product. Each participant left the two-day residential having benefited from the space, time and support, each having developed the writing they came with. Each also left with new ideas developed by working with others; for example, where to try to publish, or how to change the focus or language to address a different audience. This meant that the writing was not just further on, or completed, in this time and space but was enhanced, as it was more developed, more critical and more polished. Several writers kept in touch with their writing partner after the residential and some of the group met to review progress some months after. All found the experience beneficial in building the confidence and practice of being scholarly or academic writers. To date, four articles have been published since attending the writing residential.

In each of the three examples writing has supported professional development through collaboration, sharing ideas and challenging existing assumptions about who can be a writer and what they should produce. Writing has been understood as a social activity which is supported through a process of thinking, talking and listening. These are activities that relate to who we are, our history, culture and our future, not simply to learning disembodied skills.

Part Three

Meanings, applications and approaches: Recommendations to practitioners

Introduction to Part Three

Having presented four case studies from practice, this section takes the reader through a process of deconstruction and reconstruction to show how each applies and exemplifies what we propose in our model. We then consider how this may be applied. Part Three begins by drawing together the case studies and concepts by unpacking the processes within our model. We refer back to elements discussed earlier, returning to and applying our model using the concept of professional capital, enabling structures and learning spaces to discuss ideas for implementation within organisations and by individuals. Together, the two chapters that make up this final section build on exemplars of practice supported by ideas drawn from our experience and explain how our model for critical professional development can be used.

In the first chapter we look at how professional learning takes place through enabling structures and learning spaces in practice using our case studies. We discuss each in turn to illustrate development and the use of spaces and structures; from the wider context, within and across organisations and at an individual level. We talk about how professionals learn within these spaces and unpack how they can therefore build components of critical professionalism, arguing for the value of what emerges through enhanced professional capital.

Development is shown to respond to external policy drivers, to perceived need, individual experimentation, or a combination of factors. The case studies show how some activity may be formally managed whilst other activities are informal and more practitioner-based. Together, they show a range of possibilities, which in most cases and to some degree enable change and professional development. In each, this process has added to the professional capital of individuals, organisations, professional bodies and the field of education more widely. Whilst the 'impact' of each is difficult to measure, and simple performance indicators are to be avoided (Ball, 2003), each author shows clearly the relevance, purpose and significance of their work to students, themselves and colleagues within a teaching and learning nexus (Jenkins and Healey, 2005).

In the closing chapter we draw together the threads in the book to introduce and discuss approaches for the reader to consider in their practice. The emphasis shifts to ways that professional learning can be purposefully constructed and enabled by organisations and within wider contexts. We return to our model from Chapter Two and use this to discuss the way learning space and enabling structures can be enacted across organisations and linked to the wider context. In this respect we are shifting from professional learning focusing on the individual to a development perspective directed at organisational enablers. These enablers may be teacher educators, senior managers, policy makers, policy implementers, or human resource managers. We close the book with a discussion of the role played by this group in framing and shaping the learning spaces and enabling structures for critical professional development; they are crucial in decision making and adapting our model to suit the needs of the respective settings and organisational context.

This shift in focus allows us to discuss a sustained and sustainable developmental approach that is equally beneficial to the organisation and the individual. We argue that the model has the potential to have an impact on the learning experience for students and staff, as well as the capacity of the organisation to deliver high-quality learning in and across a range of settings. We link this to developing strategies and approaches for individuals and for organisations using mini-examples of practice to show how this might be achieved.

CHAPTER SEVEN

Unpacking the case studies

Introduction

Here, we discuss the case studies in more detail. In each we will be revisiting elements of the model for supporting critical professional development, analysing how the examples apply underlying principles and requirements raised earlier. To do this we revisit the concept of professional capital and the principles supporting our model shown in Chapter Two. We suggest there that professional capital is underpinned by several propositions:

1. The first sees the professional as an individual who learns best through social, discursive and reflective processes structured in and around practice.
2. The second argues for progressive structures to support identity creation in a way that reflects role, career stage and personal and professional need.
3. The third interrogates what counts as educational knowledge, questioning 'Whose knowledge?' and 'How is it acquired and developed?'
4. The fourth acknowledges that professional learning is situated within organisations, practices and processes, and in order to be critical has to embrace wider political and professional contexts.
5. The fifth emphasises the necessity for designing purposeful and embedded approaches to professional learning that maximise critical learning opportunities and acknowledge interrelationships between stakeholders and their interests.

We identify the learning spaces and enabling structures generated within each case study example to illustrate, in concrete terms, responses from our everyday practices that are meeting challenges and creating opportunities for professional learning. We discuss how each case study applies the model, exploring the extent to which the interventions are organisation-, individual- or policy-led, examining the nature of the spaces and structures that are generated. To do this we re-visit the model illustrated and discussed earlier (Figure 7.1).

The case studies exemplify in a variety of ways how workshops, training, courses and networks have been constructed and influenced by different sets of interrelationships between the individual, the organisation and the wider field. For each this is dependent upon the context, purpose, structures and spaces that are available and that can be utilised and developed. As we comment earlier, it is impossible to have a 'one size fits all' model, as individual activity occurring within learning spaces

Figure 7.1 Our model for supporting critical professionalism using enabling structures and learning spaces

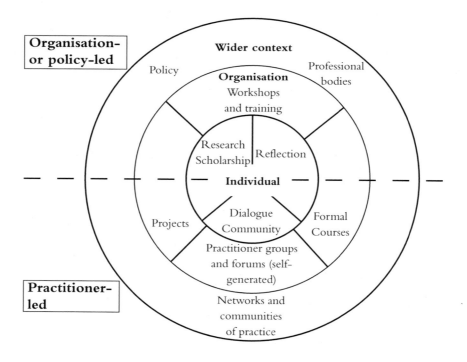

and supporting structures are context-, time- and resource-bound. To illustrate this we return to our definition of critical professionalism to highlight the extent to which each case study differently addresses the preconditions or supports the behaviours of critical professionalism. What we find is that there are shared components of critical profession-alism across all case studies, and also that particular contexts influence and support specific characteristics more than others. This reinforces our experience that critical professionalism has to be viewed in terms of career paths, emergent and dynamic identity and practice, and as both initial and continuing professional learning.

Our definition of critical professionalism, discussed earlier, requires educational practitioners to:

- possess an appreciation of one's own professional capital and how to develop and apply it;
- identify and use selectively opportunities for learning purposefully to enhance self and practice, becoming a learning professional;
- learn through critical reflection that is informed by values, wider understanding, scholarship, reflection on practice and inter-rogation of own assumptions and prior learning;
- become skilled in the multiple discourses that enable operation across diverse communities for the purpose of sustaining and creating professional identity;
- develop awareness of the complex state and interplay of know-ledge and practice;
- apply agency within the organisational context to make judge-ments and initiate actions on one's own and others' behalf with respect to practice, position and career.

In the first case study, Lynne Barnes explores how establishing a deaf and British Sign Language teaching award acts as a formal learning space. This case study can clearly be located within the formal courses area of our model. It shows that even when working from the inside out, from within a specific organisation outwards to the wider field and awarding bodies, individual reflection at the centre of our model is needed. It illustrates the value and contribution of project initiatives as enablers in designing spaces and structure for developing critical professionalism.

In the second case study, Ruth Pilkington's description of a progression framework for continuing professional development is also located with the formal courses area in the model. This focuses specifically on the development of characteristics of critical professionalism as a function of continuing professional education. In this case study the scholarly practitioner, developed within and across the organisation-led circle, is supported through dialogue and within a scholarly community which sits at the centre of our model. It shows how a course can be designed specifically as an enabling structure.

In the third case study, Christine Hough examines how to develop critical thinking in her early years students, a key characteristic for empowerment and agency in the critical professional working in this sector. Working from policy to practice shows a movement from the outside in. Here, analysing policy and official documentation, located in the wider context, occurs in the workshop and training area of the model. This case study, and the examples within it, shows the centrality of reflection at all stages of developing critical professionalism.

In the fourth case study, Yvon Appleby discusses using writing to develop academic and professional capital. This work is located in the practitioner groups and forums area of the model, relying on self-selection and networks to promote and support activity. It shares some elements of project activity in its exploration of the contribution made by bounded, purposeful and defined activity. As such it is different to the other three case studies which rely on more formal spaces and structures. In this study the emphasis is on individually led activity built around research and scholarship, which sit at the heart of the model. The activities take place within groups and processes where talk plays an important part in the generation of ideas but the learning activity is structured around creating space for individual writing. To explore how each aspect of professional development works with and across the parts of our model we discuss the case studies separately.

Applying the model of critical professional development to our case studies

Case study 1: Training deaf people to teach

The development of the formal programme described in Chapter Three, leading to a recognised teaching award, responds to difficulties deaf individuals experience in becoming a BSL teacher. Here we have an excluded community – excluded through language, part-time working, funding and the existing delivery of professional development programmes. Traditionally, as discussed, the vast majority of BSL teachers come into the role by chance, often lacking educational and academic experience. The majority of BSL teachers may have specific language expertise, as native speakers, but are otherwise non-traditional learners and are not trained in how to teach others. Individual practitioners therefore experience difficulties operating and being accepted as professional teachers, affecting both identity and confidence, and their professional capital.

The programme, unlike previous training available to the community, provides a learning space for individuals to learn within a BSL dialogic community: the deaf students' first language. By being able to communicate and learn through shared experiences, deaf students are enabled to engage in more nuanced and critical reflection, in marked contrast to previous experiences of simply 'having to learn on the job'. The case study identifies the particular value this process has for BSL practitioners because of the importance of beginning with practical concrete experience in their knowledge construction. Delivering the programme in BSL to native speakers reduces the individual isolation experienced within previous 'cultures of silence' enabling deaf students to become first-hand learners rather than recipients of third- hand or translated information. The BSL teacher training course emerged from a project initiative that was prompted as a response to the needs of individuals and of policy requirements for a qualified workforce; consequently it bridges several elements of our model.

By structuring a space which supports learning through reflection, scholarship and dialogue, the BSL teacher training course responds to the individual at the heart of our model. It adds pedagogic understanding to existing subject knowledge and supports purposeful deliberative reflection which is fundamental to the learning of educational professionals, thereby empowering the practitioners from the BSL community. The programme provided a unique opportunity for practitioners to learn through peer support, enabling discussion and assessment of their own learning process as well as their teaching methods and approaches. In this way, the trainee teachers, some for the first time, were able to become critical and reflective learners.

In response to policy and wider requirements, the programme provides structure, support and space for deaf individuals to develop the skills and knowledge necessary to become qualified professional teachers addressing the broader context. The development of the programme responds to the gap between the needs of deaf individuals and provision of teaching of BSL in further and higher education more generally. The changes in 2007 to the national requirements for further education teachers, referred to in the case study, meant that BSL teachers needed to gain nationally recognised qualifications, providing added impetus to the design and delivery of the course. These two needs (individual and the wider context) are mediated through the programme in the learning spaces and enabling structures developed to support learning and critical professional development for deaf BSL teachers.

In designing the structures and spaces in the programme, consideration had to be given to delivery through targeting needs and meeting specific requirements of students which results in a genuinely inclusive learning space. This in practice meant responding to students who are largely teaching part-time by offering block teaching supported with online and blended learning. The delivery, designed around these accessible enabling structures and learning spaces, focused on the deaf students' needs rather than developing a 'BSL adapted' existing model. In this way, the central individual elements of the model meet the characteristics for development as critical professionals: complexity of practice, discourses and reflective learning.

The need to create a qualification-awarding programme for deaf teachers working in further education clearly responds to the way in which spaces in the outer circle in our model are shaped by policy drivers as the impetus for change. These policy drivers, impacting upon deaf teachers as upon others, provided the rationale for changes in further education which moved to professionalise a workforce that the case study shows was 'under-qualified at best, de-professionalised through no fault of their own'. What the outer circle space does not show is *how* this is structured and implemented. The programme emerges as an immediate response to policy change but also potentially has long-term, ongoing impact for its participants through the network that developed around it.

By working through and across circles in our model the complex interrelationships at play around the programme can be viewed both individually and as a whole. As a whole, the programme emerges as a significant force for an initial teacher training qualification and for the professional development of deaf teachers in further education. At an individual and group level, mentoring networks, designed to provide individual support, are consolidated through the subsequent embedding within professional groups beyond the course. Individuals may themselves become role models for other deaf students who may see a career in teaching BSL as a viable professional option. This case study shows the different elements acting and reacting in the development of qualified deaf teachers in the further education sector. It started with a policy initiative and was implemented through a student-responsive programme that supported the development of individual and collective professional identity and capital. By looking at the whole picture, made up of the different elements, the case study shows the relationship of each element to another rather than a series of separate and independent activities and actions. The models of professional development we discussed earlier in Chapter One – identified as knowledge, career and doing and becoming – are useful but also leave some gaps in this example. Whilst the deaf students have knowledge of their sign language subject, as non-traditional learners they have little knowledge of learning themselves. This suggests a limitation for these students in, for example, Shulman's (1987) categories of professional knowledge, as he identifies general pedagogic knowledge as well as learners' characteristics. These are experiences and knowledge the students do not have available to draw upon. The assumption of prior knowledge of learning is characteristic of other theories in this model (cf. Barnett and Coate, 2001; Fichtman and Yendol Hoppey, 2008). This is also a difficulty with simply applying a career model of professional development as, clearly, many deaf teachers have limited career opportunities, previously being seen to be subject experts in sign language rather than professional teachers. The notion of apprenticeship is also problematic, as what is described in the case study shows individual pathways with little mentoring or access to experienced deaf teachers. The doing and becoming model, with its emphasis on learning, provides a more useful way of considering the initial teacher training and continuing professional development of deaf teachers in this sector. The programme, with critical self-reflection supported through peer support and dialogue, has an awareness of the social construction of deaf people and of the construction of context-specific, time-bound teaching identities. It enables the teachers, once qualified, to continue their progress in Billett's words of 'always becoming' (in Robson, 2006: 73) in an ever-changing sector.

The formal programme, responding to requirements from policy and professional bodies, has created professional opportunities for individuals and the foundations of a professional group endowed with professional capital. Whilst previously this group of teachers remained second-hand learners who were ill-equipped as critical practitioners or subject specialists, the programme has created the baseline conditions for the individual practitioner to become and develop as a critical professional. Whilst external initial teacher training qualification requirements may change in the future, this case study shows how organisationally enabling structures and learning spaces can support the development of critical professional deaf sign language teachers. This is based upon a pedagogic response to the learning needs of the students, supporting critical reflection and early professional development rather than simply training to achieve qualification required at a policy level.

The first characteristic of our definition of critical professionalism can be applied to this case study where individuals, through the programme, can potentially **possess an appreciation of their professional capital and how to develop and apply it**.

We conclude that there is significant potential value for the individual participants and the employing institutions as a result through the acquisition of professional capital (see Table 7.1).

Understanding this may help to enhance the opportunity for BSL practitioners and course providers in developing further professional capital, individually and organisationally. Being able to communicate the advantages of formal professional development to different audiences may be increasingly significant as external drivers change opportunities available to individuals and organisations.

Table 7.1 Summary of the benefits of critical professionalism

Benefits to individuals:	Benefits to employers:
Increased sense of agency	Satisfied and engaged workforce
Employability	Harmonisation of competing agendas
Collaboration and networking	Staff as co-creators and directors in
Refreshment and motivation	their own CPD through the network

Case study 2: A progression framework for formal continuing professional education

This second case study offers explicit links to the model and to the definition of a critical professional. The concept of a critical professional is central to the programme, as suggested by the namesake module described in it. The individual practitioner sits at the heart of the award framework and the spaces and structures have clearly been designed to develop characteristics of critical professionalism through dialogue, the community environment, reflective processes and research. It is evident that practitioners are well motivated to engage with the programme for this reason, as their comments suggest, although they also speak of finding it at times a challenging journey. Research is discussed in some detail using the concept of the 'scholarly practitioner' and in the context of leadership and contribution to the professional knowledge base, spanning the professional development timeline. The concept offers strong links with communities of practice and a shared knowledge base, as outlined in Part One of this book.

This programme is different from continuing professional development opportunities which are sometimes offered within organisations and which do not provide well-structured developmental learning. The framework as a whole creates a formal, bounded and legitimate space for learning accommodating two components of professional learning: the fact that practitioners are constantly learning, acquiring new knowledge and skills, in and for their work; and that professionals learn through deliberative, informed processes of critical reflection. The central and individual part of our model is shaped in this case study by the spaces of the next circle, defined as organisation-led, which here relates to formal courses. The formal course develops new practitioner knowledge and insight rather than simply teaching existing ideas. Significantly, practitioners can interrogate existing practice discursively informed by theoretical concepts and scholarship. This is supported by the key principles of module development which use a staged progression based upon a conceptual framework of dialogue, professional engagement and scholarly practice. The learning spaces created within the formal courses, which are facilitated and mediated, are designed to be safe and collegial, allowing for exploration and discovery through dialogue and professional connection with others. The practice focus of assignments also supports criticality and acknowledges the centrality of practice as a 'locus for professional learning'. The course structure enables progression.

The learning space described in this second case study is organisation-led and organisationally aligned in that the practitioners are researching and exploring their practice, all of which occurs within the organisation and in the practitioner's work. As a consequence, it unites the situated nature of professional learning, a practice focus through doing, and space to foster critical perspectives on identity. The work space, or practice context, therefore becomes a learning space, supported through the formal courses benefiting the organisation by enhancing quality and expertise. The course acts as a safe enabling structure supporting the staged development of applied, practice-oriented, practitioner knowledge which adds to the professional capital of the individual and the organisation. The development of practice communities within the framework enables sharing knowledge within and across institutions, and in some cases between further and higher education organisations. The example given in the case study is of a joint conference called 'sharing practice', which all participants are invited to present or attend, and of learning sets in modules which work across sectors and organisations in the masters programme.

The two examples, course and community, together form an enabling structure and learning space. They are shaped by what we refer to in our model as the wider context. In this case study the formal accredited courses within the framework respond to external professional bodies, in turn influenced by educational policy. Drawing upon the SEDA Professional Development Framework, the courses respond to the move towards professional qualification for teachers in both higher and further education. As we discuss in Chapter One, teachers in further education have been required to obtain nationally recognised qualifications and until recently to undertake 30 hours continuing professional development to maintain a licence to practise. The accredited courses within the framework provide an opportunity for individuals to engage with continuing professional development that is meaningful, creating a path for further development benefiting practice and the organisation. In higher education the courses provide clear pathways, for example the postgraduate certificate in learning and teaching in higher education (LTHE) for acknowledging and accrediting the practice of teaching and scholarship in higher education. In the example of the case study, the flexible practice-based focus for learning means the individual can explicitly utilise learning drawn from and developed within the community contact space of the course, applying it critically to their individual practice.

The formal learning space provided within the accredited courses provides an additional method for development, one which by its enabling structure and content can support individual critical professional development. The comments from the students describe this learning as powerful, helping to achieve insight into a 'real world' understanding of education as it is lived by those who invest in it daily. The knowledge and understanding generated through the accredited courses does not simply stay with the individual informing their practice as it is shared at conferences and in articles intended for wider audiences. The knowledge, whilst being applied, practice-oriented practitioner knowledge, is informed by theory and critical discussion within the courses and underpinning dialogic processes. Vloet, Jacobs and Veugelers (2013) capture this well: 'Professional development can be seen as social spaces and interactive processes in which experiences are shared, differences are explored, meanings are constructed and actions are taken' (p. 420).

This case study illustrates how our understanding of the critical professional is informed by models of curriculum development and reflection. As we discuss in Chapter One, and drawing upon Van Manen's work (1991), in order to achieve a transformative level of reflection the case study shows that reflection needs direction and to be informed by critical, interrogatory engagements.

The second characteristic of our definition of critical professionalism can be applied to this case study where individuals, through the continuing professional development framework, can potentially **identify and use selectively opportunities for learning purposefully to enhance self and practice, becoming a learning professional.**

This case study, perhaps more deliberately than the first, utilises the learning space to generate opportunities for developing perspectives and all aspects of the critical professional. This is appropriate for those who are more experienced and at a different stage in their career, with a wider experience of learning. It is evident from the purposeful structuring of the learning space and enabling of development that the participants on the programme are encouraged to exercise choice, are engaging with wider perspectives and knowledge to develop their praxis, and are increasingly conceptualised as empowered and as agents of change. This is identified as an explicit goal of research activity for the scholarly practitioner and is central to the EdD. It is strengthened by the focus on continuing professional development rather than a one-off teacher training and is embedded through networks, sharing events and by the final progression towards the professional doctorate award.

Learning is a central aspect of this case study; this is more than knowledge acquisition or developing pedagogic expertise. As practitioners navigate their way through the different modes of knowledge, from the disciplinary and technical in modes 1 and 2, to more applied and critical knowledge in modes 3 and 4, they are engaged in what Eraut (1994) calls deliberative reflection. As professionals they are making choices about their individual workplace professional development. In this case they are accessing it through a formal course structure which, supported by critical reflection, enhances confidence and affects practice. Becoming an enhanced learning professional, and being recognised as such within an organisation, supports career development and potential further progression within the framework.

There are drawbacks, however, as the case study prompts questions about the implications of funding for a formal course. A formal route to development is linked to visible cost. Here, the concept of professional capital is of value as it allows the framing of development as significant, value-adding and linked to quality – particularly in connection with delivery of the student experience and educational effectiveness. Whilst clearly benefiting the individual as well as their professional capital, the case can be made that a formal framework provides high-quality learning opportunities that will benefit the organisation directly in changes to procedures and practice.

Case study 3: Bringing about the shift from knowledge acquisition to critical thinking in higher education students

In introducing our model we suggest that in order to be critical, professional learning has to embrace wider political and professional contexts. We emphasise that it is necessary to design purposeful and embedded approaches to professional learning that maximise critical learning opportunities which are key to the learning spaces and enabling structures in our model. In its discussion of how an undergraduate module is supporting the development of critical thinking for students on a Children, Schools and Families degree programme, the third case study illustrates ways that these principles can be accommodated. It addresses the challenge of engaging with and applying policy to practice faced by undergraduates working in early years settings, and describes a series of teaching interventions introduced to respond to this challenge.

Being able to interpret and evaluate policy is important for most professions, but for those working in early years settings it is arguably an essential professional skill. As policy shapes delivery of provision in the field of education, in the early years setting it also carries fast-changing legal duties and responsibilities. As the case study shows, government policy such as Every Child Matters (2003b), amendments to the Children Act (2004), and reports like the Laming Inquiry (Department of Health and Home Office, 2003) are crucial to the students' practice; yet, as discussed, many students have limited understanding of the significance or impact of these documents. Exposure to, and working with, the documentation such as serious case reviews or Ofsted reports, is not sufficient in itself to enable students to move from an initial empathetic and descriptive approach to one that critically evaluates evidence. This shows some of the difficulties with apprenticeship models which suggest that professionals learn from others in their communities of practice. It implies that experienced or long-served practitioners whom trainees learn from have relevant knowledge which can be critically applied. As such it shows the limitations of a simple career model, for those experienced practitioners, which may not underpinned by critical reflection and an awareness of policy and professional bodies.

Although there is a wide range of experience in the early years sector, overwhelmingly the case study shows that students do not automatically understand what policy is. To enable them to develop professionally, this deficiency had to be addressed as a significant part of their learning on the programme. As in the first case study, this raises questions about the previous learning experiences of the students, more than their lack of current professional knowledge. To develop as professionals they need to understand and critically apply the knowledge they were learning. Fichtman and Yendol Hoppey's (2008) distinction between knowledge *for*, knowledge *in*, and knowledge *of* practice shows the professional awareness that the students need to learn. As a response to this recognition there was an urgent need for the tutor to structure a framework within which students could interpret their work experience in terms of policies and documentation, but with a critical edge.

The undergraduate focus of the case study is particularly interesting in the context of professional education and training, which often focuses on postgraduate levels. The case study shows how the Learning from Work module acts as an enabling structure to support critical learning space for a BA degree. This represents activity within the second circle in our model, through the development of a supporting structure in the formal courses and in workshops and training. The case study provides two examples of teaching strategies used to support students in developing critical thinking skills using authentic situations and documents. These scaffold progress towards explicit learning outcomes for the module which emphasise criticality, reflection and professional behaviours. In the first, 'Susan's Story', students are asked to develop an action plan for recommended interventions for Susan and her family. Several realistic resources are provided to improve knowledge and the use of appropriate professional language. However, whilst the students' reports show that some areas and outcomes are achieved, the author in the case study describes how there was 'no evidence of links with or reference to any of the five Every Child Matters outcomes, or the specific aspects of safeguarding, as we had analysed them during the taught session'. In this respect students fail to achieve the desired critical perspective in relating policy to practice as required by the learning outcomes.

By example two in the case study, analysis of a serious case review and an Ofsted report, the students are better able to begin to make effective evaluations. This is achieved through developing an effective learning space, 'a climate', where students are given prompt phrases to articulate more critically their evaluations. This scaffolds transfer and application, which may be helpful for novice practitioners. The 'climate' is based upon an interrogation of critical thinking and learning theory. Using a revised taxonomy of the cognitive dimension of knowledge (Anderson and Krathwohl, 2001), the emphasis in the teaching and learning is relocated in active processes of creating, analysing and understanding. Rather than simply acquiring knowledge, students are required to understand it and to be able to create new understanding from it. Part of the creation of this new understanding for the students is to evaluate policy and to be able to apply this to their practice settings. For some this provides an opportunity, with management support, to introduce elements of change and professional development in their workplace. For others this is clearly more difficult as this was not positively welcomed by senior staff.

The programme illustrates the model as the design of the interventions are a response to the politically dynamic nature of the early years educational setting. At the same time they embrace the elements of the central individual circle, with its focus on dialogue, reflection and being critically informed. The module described in the programme provides a formal scaffolded structure for learning where the teaching interventions rely on application of reflection and dialogue, which lie at the heart of our model. Within the case study, students are involved in a structured process of dialogue with each other as they share knowledge and experience from their external professional communities. This is recognised by their tutor as significant for their development. As part of developing critical thinking skills students are required, through the teaching strategies, to reflect upon their previously-held assumptions of policy and to engage with the impact of their learning. This approach of starting with pre-existing knowledge characterises professional learning. The reflections of Christine, the author, show how her own critical questioning of what the students are learning, and their difficulties, supported her development of strategies for learning critical thinking skills. As she remarks, this generated a shift in her own professional perspective as she moved from teaching students 'about' policy to guiding them to a more critical stance.

The third characteristic of our definition of critical professionalism can be applied to this case study where individuals, learning critical thinking skills, can potentially **learn through critical reflection that is informed by values, wider understanding, scholarship, reflection on practice and interrogation of own assumptions and prior learning.**

Given its context and the level of study for the students, it is appropriate that this case study examines scaffolding strategies and techniques, and emphasises developing preconditions for critical professionalism and specific skills rather than targeting all aspects of the critical professionalism model. The students may not emerge as fully fledged critical professionals but the course makes a significant contribution to their capacity to develop further towards this goal. Indeed, it is evident in Christine's reflection that some students may emerge ready to engage more fully as critical professionals. At the very minimum, students will have enhanced their professional capital and added value to their employing organisations because of their increased capability to act as change agents or to apply greater criticality in their practice as a consequence of their learning. By being able to draw upon the wider policy context, rather than individual knowledge brought to the workplace by the student, change may be seen as less threatening and more about enhancing the professional capital of the organisation.

In addition, the model may support the tutor in communicating and sharing transformative elements of her module across the whole programme. The approach clearly works and would benefit the learning of other students in this sector. The outcome would be a counter to the potentially transitory impact of a single module for professionals learning early within their careers.

Case study 4: Writing as professional development

This case study introduces the role of networks and communities in supporting critical professional development. It focuses on the individual circle in our model, with its emphasis on dialogue, research, scholarship and community. It is positioned largely in the lower half of our model and, whilst it is still about enabling structures and learning space, the examples described are prompted more by individual choice than organisational requirements. The case study describes three examples of how writing can support learning or generate space for professional development.

In the first example the practitioner is enabled through the process of writing by deconstructing an area of teaching practice to support development of professional identity. The focus of the activity is to produce a book as part of a larger funded project. It is clearly about more than simply learning writing skills. The structure and the learning space engendered through the writing process support wider aspects of learning and the potential for critical professional development by writing for different audiences using peer review and critical reflection. The structure also means that group members receive some financial support, facilitated sessions and ongoing supportive critical input. Purposefully located in a higher education setting, it provides the participants with the opportunity to engage in wider discourses of academic practice and to engage with more confidence in academic writing. Developing a writing community, which has been shown by others to develop writers' identities (Murray, Stekley and MacLeod, 2012), enables the practitioners in the case study to shift from thinking that writing was something that was done by academics in university rather than by people who taught in further education. The outcome for the participants is a sense of empowerment and enhanced sense of value for their professional capital.

Writing is a key academic and professional skill, although rarely taught. In the first example, a self-selected group is given the learning space and support to develop this professional skill, helping to increase both writing competence and writing confidence. This is done through facilitation and developing discursive skills within which the enabling

144

structure encouraged discussion of 'big ideas', of critical informed reflection, and sharing practice through debate. These activities, whilst practitioner-led and using informal methods, are structured around learning through writing for the book mentioned in the case study. The first example also highlights how learning space can be enabled through critical reflection, peer discourse and support, feedback and critical questions. This relates to establishing dialogue and community in the individual area of our model. Although essentially about writing it shows clearly the role that dialogue, speaking and listening, has in contributing to critical professionalism at an individual level within a community. The example shows how developing a structured learning space around a task or process can potentially build critical professionalism, in this case challenging the power and ownership of the written word.

The second example, 'Writing about writing', also practitioner-led, was developed in response to an identified individual professional need within the postgraduate diploma programme it describes. It becomes apparent that many further education teachers on the programme lack academic and professional writing skills to act with confidence in their professional roles and in scholarly activities. The structure of the module described here develops different types of writing practice; for example, production of academic posters, peer editing, writing a professional or academic article, and writing a critical reflection. The learning space in this example, therefore, is more discrete and focused on the individual. It is also formally framed within a programme. The participants, as in the example above, learn individually but also engage in dialogue in a facilitated community, which proves a challenging but supportive space. This enabling structure encourages reflection, drawing on Brookfield's (1995) work as we discuss in Chapter One, and purposefully engages participants with wider views which include policy and the perspective of others. In this example, the practitioner is enabled through the process of writing by deconstructing an area of teaching practice to support development of professional identity. It is clearly more than simply learning writing skills and more than learning by doing – it is more about becoming and continuing to develop as Billett (2004) suggests. The semi-formal structure and the facilitated learning space support wider aspects of learning and the potential for critical professional development by writing for different audiences, including peers, students, academics and researchers. This illustrates within the model how educators belong to many professional practice communities, indicating the need to adopt an expansive learning approach for professional development. Learning and development is supported through collectivities of practice (Lindkvist, 2005) which increase individual and organisational capital.

The final example, 'Writing with and for others', represents an example of developing learning space, in this case taking the form of a writing residential for those working in higher education. The enabling structured residential provides the opportunity for individuals to focus on their own academic writing; to complete articles, finish chapters and in some cases to start new writing. Whilst individuals work on their own writing tasks, the process of reflection and review around it is facilitated using a workshop structure which is dialogic and developmental. Work and ideas are shared using paired activities and group discussion, building a 'pop-up writing culture' which, as in the two examples above, develops more than technical writing skills. It emphasises, as Illeris (2002) and Evans (2008) observe, that learning is social, emotional and cognitive: participants are motivated and have concrete objectives; the space itself is safe and constitutes a community of peers with shared interests and needs; learning is focused and targeted.

The three examples in this case study all focus on writing, and each provides a bounded, task-focused structured space. Whilst within our model this is best described as practitioner-led, and may be achieved using informal methods, the learning spaces are structured to support direction and purpose. A significant benefit in each example is that participants acquire professional capital through the structures and spaces: skills to operate more confidently as a professional or academic, to achieve external accreditation, or a significant outcome in the form of articles or a book. The case study examples each target individual rather than organisational priorities, and therefore suggest that the learning space created is one directed at experienced practitioners who choose to engage. As discussed earlier, this is a more proactive view of the career model of professional development as it relies upon individual judgement and action. Writers in the case study are potentially already operating at a level of critical professionalism, and therefore may already be **making choices to identify and use opportunities for purposefully enhancing practice.**

At the same time, the examples here meet another characteristic of our definition of critical professionalism and this therefore can be applied to this case study. It suggests that individuals, developing scholarly writing skills, can potentially **become skilled in the multiple discourses enabling operation across diverse communities for the purpose of sustaining and creating professional identity.**

All participants certainly emerge with new confidence and increased professional capital as a result of contributing through writing to an externally highly valued activity in professional life. This may require consolidation by the individuals with line managers through explicit promotion of their achievements in the context of professional capital; evidence of publication is useful reinforcement of this.

Whilst we emphasise the case studies with respect to the extent they illustrate specific factors within our definition of critical professionalism, they each also contain general factors. The sixth characteristic of our definition of critical professionalism in particular can be applied across all the case studies where individuals can potentially **develop awareness of the complex state and interplay of knowledge and practice.**

All the case studies also comply with the principles, listed at the start of this chapter, which underpin our model. This relates back to our earlier discussion of knowledge and how professionals learn, as well as the complexity and dynamic nature of education that requires engagement with both professional capital and critical professionalism. The case studies represent a range of activities in and across both further and higher education. This includes teaching strategies to promote critical thinking, developing a deaf teacher training programme, creating a continuing professional development framework, and supporting professional and academic writing through groups and projects. In each, we have explored how the model is being applied. We show that our model can support understanding the complex relations in our professional roles in the spaces projected through the interplay between the wider context, organisations and ourselves as individuals. In addition, it is helpful as an analytic and design tool. This makes it valuable for those designing and delivering learning spaces and enabling structures within any educational institution. Depending upon where the practitioner is positioned they may be engaging in a more or less active way with elements of the model. This is evident in the case studies that are being purposefully used by practitioners, are practitioner-led, or are being used for continuing professional development purposes. The capacity of practitioners to engage with their own professional capital where they acquire perspectives and behaviours of critical professionalism, at whatever stage, makes a necessary and important contribution to professionalism. In these cases, several aspects of the model are engaged with: development of capacity in case study 4; or to enhance practice and self in case study 2; and to develop fundamental characteristics in case studies 1 and 3.

The case studies inform us about the relationship between structure and agency; that is, the external factors that shape the environments we operate within, and the individual meaning and action that we undertake. This is shown in the case studies as individuals and organisations use learning spaces and enabling structures to mediate between individual, organisational and wider contextual need, interest and commitment. Figure 7.2, adapted from Figure 1.1, shows how what we describe as the component elements of critical professionalism are supported and developed through learning spaces and enabling structures. The activities we describe in the case studies enable integration and development of the component elements of critical professionalism reinforcing the value and contribution of our model.

Theoretical models and approaches, such as learning theory, reflection, professional development as career, knowledge or becoming, are evident in our case studies but they do not always explain the complex interrelationships between the individual and organisations, or how they are shaped by external drivers. As we discuss earlier, it is important for establishing the potential for critical professional development to take these interconnections into account, enabling a more nuanced picture than a simple input–output model.

Agency is a key concept in understanding and negotiating this complexity, as the case studies illustrate. Each case study in some way responds to the wider context, some more specifically and directly than others, and each operates within organisation-led spaces, some with practitioner groups and others less so. What is significant is what happens at the individual level; how agentic the individual can be. This may be dependent upon how able individuals are to talk and communicate with others, to develop a like-minded community, to share work within and across institutions, or to be able to evaluate and share what is working well or not. This is crucial to effective professional learning.

Reinforcing the importance of agency, the seventh characteristic of our definition of professionalism can be applied across all of the case

Figure 7.2 Diagram showing how case studies act as learning spaces and enabling structures to support elements of critical professionalism

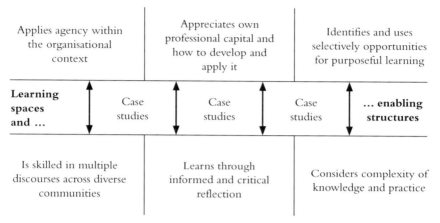

studies where individuals and groups are **able to apply agency within the organisational context to make judgements and initiate actions on one's own and others' behalf with respect to practice, position and career.**

Whilst the foundations for critical professionalism have occurred through developing learning spaces and enabling structures, there is a further step to achieving agency and active critical professionalism. Space and structures themselves do not lead to becoming critical; what happens within those spaces and structures does. Therefore, conscious and deliberative reflection before, during and after the practice described is essential. It emerges that the process of critical examination of what is at play is a fundamental component in the application of the model and in contributing to its success. This suggests facilitation and certainly reinforces the value of reflexive, informed sharing and dialogue.

As we noted in Chapter One, individuals can approach reflection as a self-referential and uninformed activity which will have little impact upon critical professional development. On the other hand, organisations may enforce management-led agendas which have little real impact upon the professional development of staff. At a time of significant change, with the establishment of new contracts in education, individuals and organisations have to find ways of establishing spaces and structures that benefit both equally. We have provided examples of this in the case studies, and in the following, concluding chapter we consider how this may be supported more widely.

CHAPTER EIGHT

Conclusions and recommendations for practice

Introduction

In this final chapter we draw together the elements of practice and theory presented in the previous sections and return to the model introduced in Chapter Two. Here, we focus on conclusions and recommendations for practitioners, targeting those in enabling roles themselves such as managers, teacher-educators, line managers, human resources practitioners, mentors and organisational change agents. Before beginning this process we return to some of the key points from earlier chapters which have particular relevance here.

The theoretical frameworks discussed in relation to the creation of professional identity, habitus, reflection and professional learning have allowed us to conceptualise the needs and issues that combine to influence the development of professional teachers and educators. Focusing on further and higher education we propose a model of critical professional development supported by two key concepts: critical professionalism and professional capital. The model underpinned by these concepts helps to explore the way that teachers might engage with their professional roles, learning and development, in what are complex, dynamic and, indeed, challenging times. In addressing this we offer:

- a definition for critical professionalism that suggests how the new professional learning and identity of practising teachers can be enacted and framed;

- a concept of professional capital which can help reframe relationships and responsibilities for employers and practitioners;
- a model for enabling the development of critical professionalism to inform the structuring of workplace learning within the organisation and for individuals.

The model centres on the generation of enabling structures and learning spaces within organisations in a way that is responsive and accommodates how professionals learn, as well as recognising organisational needs. This is a personal view, but in writing this book we have tried to make explicit the tacit 'knowing' and decisions we have made to support our work in order to present approaches and ideas that may be adaptable and applicable in a range of diverse settings.

This concluding chapter has five sections. In the first we return to the model discussed in Chapter Two to make proposals for approaches we have found particularly valuable at the three levels. These are the wider national and professional body context, the organisational context and the individual perspective. In the second section we discuss the significance of dialogue for professional development, providing short examples from practice to inform those considering its use. The third section looks at the wider professional landscape, particularly the supporting roles of professional bodies and unions in education. We suggest that the recent discourse within these larger influencing bodies can be valuable when we, as enablers, design spaces and structure for professional learning. This is particularly so in the light of the policy developments discussed in Chapter One and later in this chapter. The fourth section offers a practical method to support professional development which enables professional capital for individuals and organisations. It pulls together the discussion on learning space and enabling structures to propose an organisation-wide approach which is founded on the concepts discussed throughout this book. The last section looks at the use of facilitation in developing and working with enabling structures and learning spaces.

Developing a model for critical professionalism

In the first section of the book we set out the theoretical framework for our model. In Chapter One, we focused on the setting, discussing the complexity of the context for education across all sectors but primarily focusing on post-compulsory and higher education. It is clear

152

that education is now firmly established in a state of complexity and change where the competitive environment is altering the ways in which we might view educational professionals in educational systems. It is evident, too, that the tensions experienced by a professional community where identity and role are tightly interconnected will continue to have an impact upon teachers. This will, we argue, generate discomfort, frustration and a sense of helplessness within individuals unless we can re-articulate what it is to be a professional educator in a positive way. We argue that whilst recognising this there are also ways of responding which can be effective in supporting education practitioners to deal with a supercomplex environment and to become an agent of action within it.

To explore the relationship between the individual and organisation in developing mutually beneficial action and agency we make use of the concept of professional capital. This allows both employing organisations and practitioners to reframe the professional areas of practice, identity and relationships. Practitioners engaging with developing their own professional capital can potentially accommodate the moral and personal drivers that brought them into the profession. This enables an agentic perspective of their individual worth and value to the organisation. As part of developing individual professional capital, practitioners can engage proactively in the necessary processes of professional decision making about career, practice and priorities. By understanding they can develop professional capital, an individual can take responsibility to be engaged, to be informed about decisions and to appreciate and respond positively to the tensions between autonomy and accountability. If practitioners do not see this as possible within the new professional contract, the danger is they will withdraw and become frustrated and increasingly stressed.

To provide a more complete picture of these interrelationships between individual and organisation, we propose that employers can use the idea of professional capital to reframe the ways that education practitioners are viewed as autonomous producers within their organisations. Teachers are primary factors within education and, as with any craft or process of production, professionally they require investments, refitting and repair. This may appear to be a functionalist portrayal of education practitioners but the organisations must, we argue, recognise how practitioners need to be supported and enabled so as to produce high-quality teaching and learning. It is at this level, the front-line, within classroom and curriculum practice, that change, innovation and quality have to be delivered. In discussing this idea in Chapter One, we suggested that organisations should acknowledge both how professional knowledge is constructed and the nature of the educational professional. Without time and space in practice, processes and environments practitioners cannot make their experiential knowledge work in producing good learning for their students.

In examining the recent developments at national level in terms of professionalism, we note how the requirement in higher education for organisations to be active in the development of professional capacity is being recognised within the new professional standards framework. This increases expectations for organisations to lead continuing professional development for teaching and learning roles. Organisations might use our approaches in acknowledging their role in initial and continuing professional development and learning reflecting our view that 'education practitioners need to reflect in order to learn, make sense of their knowing and to perform effectively'.

The definition of critical professionalism in the concluding part of Chapter One summarised the factors and characteristics which need to be fostered to allow the concept of professional capital to work. It set the stage for our discussion of the model at the heart of this book. This definition informs the ways in which both the organisation and the individual practitioner need to view professional formation and development as it identifies and makes explicit the components for professional learning and the ideal characteristics for effective professionalism. We have termed our notion of professional identity and learning for educational practitioners 'critical professionalism' to make explicit the relational aspects and the importance of the conscious deliberative learning involved.

Chapter Two developed our argument for critical professionalism and professional capital from the organisational perspective, focusing on enabling the development of the critical professional within the organisation and the wider context. By examining how professionals learn best, we identified key requirements for structuring learning within organisational and sector spaces. We proposed five principles which we argue are fundamental to this process. We base our discussion on an exploration of professional learning within the literature of professional teacher identity and its formation. We link these principles to a concept of learning spaces and enabling structures to show how organisations can support professionals to meet the challenge of professional capital and sector developments. We discuss how these spaces can be structured through formal courses, projects, communities of practice and training events, also influenced by wider drivers as well as being prompted by individual practitioners themselves. In all cases, we regard these spaces as needing to accommodate the five principles supporting the individual's need to learn through dialogue within social settings and informed by scholarship and research.

In Part Two we introduced four case studies showing how the model can be applied in practice. The case studies occupy a central place as they demonstrate how, through our practice, we have been able to develop the skills and characteristics for critical professionalism in various education environments. We have used case studies that reflect the full range of opportunities within our model and its underpinning principles for critical professionalism.

In Part Three we unpack the case studies using concepts of enabling structures, learning spaces and professional capital. Following on from this, and here in our final chapter with a focus on organisations, we explore how to support critical professional development. Our model suggests that structures can be enabled and spaces created at three different levels: influenced by wider national agendas, by the organisation itself, and at individual level. Figure 8.1 reintroduces the model.

As our focus is on the organisation, we view the individual within the model as organisational agent and we concentrate on the individual in that capacity. We use examples to illustrate not only how the individual role might be enacted within the organisation but also how individual development can be facilitated. We then focus on the wider context and look at the impact and value of elements within the wider context that can be purposefully applied and developed to promote the critical professional within educational organisations. As debates around professionalism have developed, the influence of wider contexts on an organisational response to critical professionalism has also changed. To illustrate this we draw on the contributions and recommendations of unions and on the example of national professional bodies. Additionally, we reflect on the value of national project contributions whose influence, whilst directed at student learning, informs professional need and organisational development. Finally, we offer a proposal for an organisation-wide application of enabling structures and learning spaces. We visit Dewey Educational Institution, a fictitious creation, to illustrate this. It shows how enabling structures and learning spaces can be embedded within an organisation.

155

Figure 8.1 Revisiting the model for supporting critical professional development

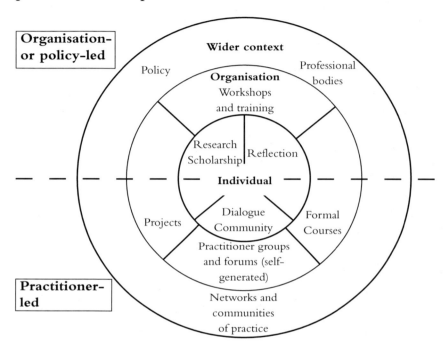

The agentic individual

According to our model at the individual level the practitioner can draw on reflection, dialogue, research and scholarship as tools for developing her/himself as a critical professional. These tie in closely to the two core factors of our definition of critical professionalism, namely that the critical professional:

- is skilled in multiple discourses across diverse communities;
- learns through informed and critical reflection.

The latter notion of informed and critical reflection emphasises an active approach in the individual's own learning and development. It is one that seeks to problematise practice and to inform solutions and understanding by application of research and scholarship. This is illustrated in the case studies. It is an approach that involves a critical appraisal and reappraisal of one's own tacit knowledge and assumptions. We suggested the idea of purposive and purposeful reflection on practice as having a critical role in individual professional learning, developed using Eraut's idea of deliberative learning in Chapter Two. This cannot happen without agency, direction and intention.

These ideas are part of what Judyth Sachs (2000) calls 'activist professionalism'. Whilst a call to individual agency and action is positive, there is, however, a challenge with this concept. It relies primarily on the individual's ability to exploit spaces (gaps) and interstices (Groundwater-Smith and Sachs, 2002) and to resist the excesses of an audit culture. This is not always possible and lays considerable burden on the individual. The notion of critical professionalism that we adopt recognises this challenge and suggests that for the individual there are organisational structures and spaces within normal workplace activity and processes. These can and should be exploited as they allow dialogue to take place, critical reflection to occur and practice to be interrogated and more widely informed. Such spaces are illustrated in the small examples below:

Example 1: Sharing practice through a masters project

Recognising that part-time teachers studying at masters level would struggle to balance busy workloads and their study during the final research project, we designed regular contact workshops to support the research process – ethics, approval, planning and data collection, and write up. This means that participants from a wide range of sectors are able to use the workshops to share, explore, critique and discuss their own work, learn from others and manage their research. It has resulted in the development of a community of practitioner-researchers who have gained value from dialogue with peers across sectors, subjects and project topics. An outcome has been regular annual events at which research is disseminated and shared using posters.

Example 2: Vocational tutors benefit from professional learning space

One of the success stories for a postgraduate diploma programme for post-compulsory tutors has been to see how a group of vocational tutors, coincidentally all female, have developed confidence and skills in academic literacy through their journey to acquire teaching qualifications. Starting with certificates and progressing through PTLLS and DTLLS, these tutors have developed as a community and as individuals completing postgraduate diplomas in education. The dialogue has been rich as participants have struggled with their novice status as learners and teachers, but they have acquired a sense of belonging, authority and community in progressing their study using the course as a safe 'space' for learning and developing themselves and their practice.

In both of the above examples practitioners have sought out and used opportunities for learning which also reflect the enabling structures and learning spaces we identify in the model. In Example 1, the participants are on a course which has led them to develop possibilities for discourse, reflection and indeed scholarship around practice. Participants have chosen the course as a structured learning space which allows them to stand back from practice and devise protected space for learning and reflection. As a result they have been able to develop communities through which further discursive learning can occur. In Example 2, the practitioners are using a dialogic space framed around practice and professional standards. It is a space that has been made available to them by the organisation. The notion of dialogic space is one that is acknowledged in Senge's work on learning organisations (1990), but also sits at the heart of informal teacher education and learning (Haigh, 2005). We return to dialogue later as we explore individual learning opportunities.

The relationship between the individual and differing spaces and structures supporting formal, informal and workplace learning was introduced in Chapter One in a discussion of modes of knowledge (Scott *et al.*, 2004). According to Scott *et al.*, in modes 3 and 4, knowledge learning is constructed within and around the workplace through the actions of practitioner-researchers. Mode 3 recognises the dynamic and varied nature of workplace knowledge and therefore the limitations of formal tuition in its acquisition. Knowledge formed within the academy is seen as having less status than, or at least lagging behind, practice and therefore is viewed as inadequate. Knowledge production needs to reflect the non-predictability, situation-specificity and the contextualised nature of practice as relevant workplace knowledge. Within

158

this conceptualisation of practice-based knowledge the individual may draw on academic knowledge as a resource but the academy cannot fully answer practice questions. It is important, therefore, that the individual recognises her or his own values, using them to decide on the fit of knowledge and academic processes to practice. Knowledge-formation as a consequence becomes a deliberative process of determining answers *in situ*, reminiscent of Eraut (2004).

Mode 4, primarily about criticality, emphasises the significance of the workplace setting with the aim of exposing power whilst exploring practice in situations and contexts. It is significant to note that such things are not always desirable or welcome. Mode 4 knowledge is about change interventions as it is founded on a critique of assumptions of knowledge requiring values-checking and interrogation. In our exploration of critical professionalism, modes 3 and 4 can be interpreted as informing and constructing thinking about the individual in practice seeking to create professional knowledge. These modes of knowledge recognise and reinforce that knowledge-creation has to take place within the workplace through purposive interrogation of existing knowledge and process, and the deliberative creation of new professional, practice knowledge. The complex positioning of the practitioner within practice, political and wider contexts is fundamental to how mode 4 knowledge is conceptualised. This view highlights the importance of critical reflexivity in the process of individual knowledge production which we suggest takes place through research, workplace learning and scholarship. The process of mode 4 knowledge production is particularly relevant for the learning and knowledge construction of practitioners who learn in and through practice, but there is a caveat: for it to be successful, it requires space and time within organisational and teaching processes to make knowledge productive. This is illustrated in a third short example:

Example 3: The professional doctorate in education
The purpose of this intervention has been to develop a doctorate which targets specifically the needs of professional educators in full-time work wishing to explore and develop their professional knowledge at a high level. It recognises that mid- or late-career professionals bring significant expertise and professional experience to doctoral study but they may need support to manage the process of doctoral work, to

develop the specific research skills and competences which also form part of doctoral authority and recognition. One of the key challenges for course team and participants is to develop ways and means of engaging reflexively in the challenge of creating professional knowledge that is highly contested, critical and power-laden. Participants use dialogue, peer reflection, metaphor and writing exercises to develop some of these skills.

Increasingly, as our short examples show, practitioners enter education through initial teacher education and see further courses as a means of developing necessary career skills, and even as a necessary continuing support. The current drive at national levels for professional qualifications has added impetus and value to such courses. Within higher education there has been a significant growth in postgraduate qualifications targeting the continuing professional development of practitioners in all sectors. The concept of critical professionalism provides a natural focus for curriculum design of such programmes that complements this trend and also reflects professional standards. It is imperative that employers recognise the worth of such 'spaces' as valid mechanisms through which quality of teaching can be enhanced and developed.

The case for professional dialogue

Throughout, one message has been made repeatedly: the value of dialogue for the individual in supporting critical professionalism. Reflective dialogue (Eraut, 2004; Kahn *et al.*, 2006), professional talk (Cunningham, 2008), dialogue and identity (Vloet, Jacobs and Veugeler, 2013), our own processes of dialogue in constructing the models and case studies in this book – all emphasise the important contribution to learning made by dialogic process. Dialogue is central to activity of meaning-making through a process of deconstructing and reconstructing practice, trying to articulate the tacit 'known' so it can become shared and valuable to the community. The discursive process of professional identity creation with policy, around practice, and with the different communities that form part of the professional landscape has been developed in the research of Brookfield (1995), Barnett (2008) and Ligorio and Cesar (2013) which we have drawn on in earlier chapters. The naturally occurring professional conversations that we have in practice, however, can fail to contribute to learning without some element of directed reflection as we suggest. This is reinforced by work undertaken by Haigh (2005), by Cunningham (2008) and by Pilkington (2013) and may form part of individual review of teaching, mentoring, learning sets, courses, and even assignment activity as we suggest earlier. The important thing is that it must be directed or, as Eraut (2004) suggests, made deliberative and purposive. This, we propose, can be achieved through what we have termed professional dialogue, and this section discusses how a formalised professional dialogue can function at the individual level of our model and provide a fundamental basis for professional learning across courses, projects, in workplace processes, and within communities of practice.

Example 4: The professional standards dialogue

This formally structured dialogue has been developed as a means of making evident the learning and experience of professional higher education practitioners for the purpose of granting accreditation using the UK professional standards framework (PSF). Descriptor 2 of the standards focuses on the core role of the lecturer in higher education and requires evidence of meeting all dimensions within the framework. Through a series of structured, formal, mentor-led dialogues, lecturers are supported to make their tacit knowledge about teaching, learning and assessment practice visible and to explore it within a professional context in order to achieve professional accreditation. The approach has emerged as rigorous, flexible and affirmatory for participants.

The example above introduces the use of dialogue for recognising and awarding professional status for experienced professional teachers. This approach is a valuable one for organisational facilitators to emulate for purposive development. The dialogue example uses a framework of professional standards statements to structure dialogues between a mentor and an experienced practitioner. This process focuses specifically upon experienced practitioners because for them the workplace setting has been the main focus for their professional learning and experience. Courses may be less appealing to established practitioners who feel they are sufficiently 'expert'. The dialogue structures a progressive unpacking of practice informed by professional standards statements, culminating in recognition of professional status. It is facilitated by a mentor but may equally be facilitated by a critical partner, manager or through a team activity. In the example given above, a mentor introduces the process. It is supported by documentation that includes a review of practice mapped against the standards, and a minimum of three dialogues take place. These explore how the individual is applying values and areas of knowledge identified within the standards statement within her or his practice or workplace setting. A final 'assessed' dialogue involving a third person from outside the practitioner's practice setting adds rigour and provides a means of formally recognising, sharing and celebrating the individual's professionalism. A detailed account of this dialogue can be found at www.escalate.ac.uk/6333. This model of professional dialogue has been developed from a decade of experience using dialogue as an assessment tool in professional learning awards. It is informed by the theoretical approach proposed in Brockbank and McGill (1998) and is summarised in research into dialogue by Pilkington (2013). Within the course of a structured, professional dialogue, learning for participants develops over time through the dialogic process and as both mentor and mentee input varies in emphasis and input. The outcome of the process is learning for all participants: mentor, mentee and ultimately the organisation, because the sharing of practice contributes to the knowledge base for the community of practice in the organisation.

The key to making a professional dialogue work is to focus it around the individual's own process of meaning making and articulation of tacit understandings developed in practice. It synthesises widely accepted components of professional knowing such as knowledge, values and practice, allowing development around Barnett and Coate's model of curriculum (2001) of knowledge, action and self, discussed earlier. In the role of the mentor, we envisage a person experienced in understanding the meaning of professionalism espoused by the established professional body and in the local practice and organisational context of the individual practitioner. The mentor is able to share common ideas and experiences and also assists in the translation of the tacit 'knowns' into the literacy and framework of the professional body. This supports the meta-cognitive and reflective process for the individual practitioner as the mentor facilitates a supportive dedicated space for the individual practitioner allowing for rigorous exploration, probing and challenge. The ownership of the process, however, sits with the mentee-practitioner who, in the professional dialogue, carries a responsibility for continuing the dialogue and reflective process outside the actual timed conversation.

This is done through notes and reflections and, whilst brief, provides support and evidence for the structuring of a final assessed dialogue. The aim is to generate a deliberative process of reflection and learning framed within a specific professional context, providing time and space for this within the practitioner's work. It also provides professional input from a critical and supportive, experienced 'other', facilitating development and engagement with the wider contexts, knowledge and practice.

This type of structured dialogue can support the development of critical professionalism where it is applied in practice settings. It can be adapted using learning sets allowing group development and reflection. It can support structured dialogue within and around practice activity such as course review, continuing professional development, appraisals and peer observation of teaching. Critical to the success of the professional dialogue process is the role of an experienced facilitator and also a structure and framework through which dialogue can be guided. This is where the concept of critical professionalism is useful. In implementing professional dialogue as a targeted development approach, organisations can draw on the wider context; for example, strategic and national agendas can offer a focus for professional dialogue, as can organisational priorities and, of course, individually-led objectives.

The wider professional landscape: Professional bodies and unions

As discussion of professionalism has developed and widened within national contexts there has been a growth in professional frameworks for each sector, national inquiry and involvement by professional bodies and unions. It is to this wider context we now turn, and to a discussion of possible resources when implementing the model for critical professional development. These resources are national projects, unions and professional bodies.

Projects and networks
We suggest in our model that projects perform particularly well as learning spaces and enabling structures. They are often prompted by intense effort over a limited term and are frequently funded by organisations or by national and policy-driven initiatives. They provide task-focused spaces in which practitioners can come together purposefully to learn from each other, share practice and knowledge and develop

163

new approaches to practice in response to larger agendas and new understandings.

For us, as authors of the case studies and in the writing of this book, we have found the focused intensity of writing and the targeted dialogue, reflection and exchange highly similar to the enabling learning spaces structured by our own experiences of past projects. In reflecting on our own development we find projects have played a significant role for each of us. The case studies in Part Two provide additional evidence of how projects and national programmes can generate learning spaces. An example of this was the development in case study 1 of a national programme for BSL initial teacher training responding to the particular needs of the community for tuition and accreditation. The writing groups of case study 4 also reflect characteristics of projects in their bounded, targeted nature. Whilst space means we could not explore projects specifically in the case study chapters, nevertheless we note that projects as learning spaces are frequently initiated by both individuals and national agendas. The projects that emerge create valuable learning space for exchange and dialogue around practice, also providing enabling structures through provision of resources.

Example 5: Learning from projects
Practitioners work together on a literature review

In 2006, a group of colleagues received national funding from The Higher Education Academy to review the use of reflection on postgraduate certificates. Meetings emerged as a powerful component in the theorising and knowledge-construction process of the review team, which was a mixture of experienced researchers and practitioners.

Whilst the project was of a short duration – one year – the impact was felt by each member in an increased appreciation for the ways in which reflection could be applied and developed in their own teaching practice, and in further collaborative writing activities (Kahn *et al.*, 2006, 2008, 2009).

Creating an international sign language course

Signs2Go (2009–11) was funded by the lifelong learning programme to support the development of an international online sign language programme. It brought together teachers of signing and speaking languages from across

Europe, something that might not otherwise have happened. Opportunities emerged through workshops for collaboration and exchanges on teaching experiences and cultural pedagogy. The social, cultural and professional exchanges around the project meetings and events provided a valuable learning experience for all participants and fed into further development of social spaces for deaf practitioner participants when constructing professional knowledge (Hessman and Pyfers, 2013).

Teaching Fellow grants and awards
The small pots of funding granted by organisations to reward teaching excellence can be used in a variety of ways. One teaching fellow used a small award to fund a review of assessment practice across a faculty and then to set up a series of events and workshops to explore and discuss findings. The resultant sharing and exchange supported small follow-on projects to enhance assessment activity by individuals, to disseminate outcomes across the faculty and led to a burgeoning of innovation and enhancement (Pilkington, 2006).

In taking this forward into recommendations for practitioners, it is clear that projects have a particular value as a learning space and in enabling exchange and development for educational practitioners. That they are often prompted by national agendas means that elements of critical professionalism can emerge as a natural consequence of any development experienced by participants through their engagement in the wider context and its application to practice. We present several factors at national levels that have been particularly useful in developing learning spaces for critical professionalism to be supported.

The move to professionalise post-compulsory education has enabled the growth of national networks, groups around projects, national initiatives and research in subject areas, for example. These to some extent resemble 'collectivities of practice' (Lindkvist, 2005) in that they offer a self-generated community environment in which teachers can pursue self-development. This can be an individual choice, so they are suitable for individuals seeking professional development, and are more relevant to the needs of engaged critical professionals rather than developing critical professionalism. Another example within higher education is The Higher Education Academy which provides a network and access point for other networks to develop around 'special interest groups' and the opportunity to bid for short-term project funding. Throughout three decades there has been targeted use of subject and thematic networks, funding provision and increased use of virtual lists through which individuals can access communities of practice to promote development of teaching and learning. One of the most useful facilities for professional networking is the use of Joint Information Systems Committee (JISC) lists, now being supplemented by Facebook, Twitter feeds and the growing use of on-line discussion groups. The shift within higher education to develop a professional approach to teaching is a good example of how concerted effort across a sector has been applied and has influenced organisational change. Without the significant investment nationally in The Higher Education Academy and the development of a professional standards framework, the growth and existence of networks would not have been available for individuals in higher education. Similarly, the simple existence of professional standards has made real the allocation of resources and time to development at organisational level. The impact of national initiatives and anticipated changes for the post-compulsory sector was discussed in Chapter One.

Professional bodies and unions

The changing landscape at a national level has stimulated corresponding wider interest in communities of practice, the concept of professional identity and its support by unions and other professional organisations. This is reflected in the fact that the University and College Union (UCU) has issued statements and discussion documents on the topic of professionalism, what it is to be a professional in the view of the union, and how it might be supported. The UCU consultation document 'Towards a UCU Policy on Professionalism' (2013) touches on some of the concepts within our model. It highlights the fact that professional identity requires new forms of professionalism and engagement which should be active. It recognises the fact that discussion of an activist professional identity (Sachs, 2000) allows communities of practice to develop, seeing the purpose of these communities as environments through which critical pedagogies can be developed and enhanced. Furthermore, it recognises that professionals must engage with the wider contexts in which they work, where any formal policy for professionalism must recognise that education engenders a multiplicity of identities and professionalisms. Such national statements are important tools which organisations and critical professionals can, and should, use in the development of individual capacity and practice.

There are other resources nationally that can be used in more practical ways. Whilst national agendas influence development indirectly, providing fertile ground for growing and sustaining learning spaces, there are a number of national certifications and award providers through which critical professionalism can be supported and which can frame organisational learning space. Professional standards developments in both further and higher education have stimulated the introduction of specific programmes and certificates providing valuable early-career learning spaces in the form of courses and the requirement to attend. In case study 2, for example, we made brief reference to the Staff and Education Development Association (SEDA) as the stimulus for the development of a continuing professional development course. It is appropriate to discuss the SEDA professional development framework further here as it provides an invaluable practical resource for those seeking to frame and inform the design of continuing professional development across an organisation which develops and supports the critical professional.

SEDA's professional development framework

SEDA's professional development framework is structured around educational organisation needs in learning terms. The framework recognises that an educational organisation is not just made up of one type of professional, but many. This is evident in how the awards framework embraces development for the whole organisation. It is designed to be organisationally flexible and it recognises that individual careers within organisations progress and change around roles and function, or even the status of the individual. We interpret the value of the framework in terms of organisation learning theory in that it is a framework of awards which provides organisational 'shape' to structure and embed individual learning within an institution, and where groups of awards address particular functions in post-compulsory and higher education. Table 8.1 shows the range of awards for each organisational role (www.seda.ac.uk/ professionaldevelopment).

SEDA uses professional values statements for educational practitioners to inform all the awards within the framework. As a central core each award also uses a simple cycle of reflective experiential learning.

Table 8.1 SEDA's professional development framework showing groups of awards and links to organisational role

Awards for Academic Roles	Awards for Research Funtions	Awards for Support Functions	Awards for Development Functions
• Supporting Learning • Learning Teaching and assessing • Leading Programmes • Enhancing Academic Practice in the Disciplines • Leading and Developing Academic Practice • External Examining • Student Support and Guidance	• Supervising Postgraduate Research • Enhancing Research Practice • Action Research	• Supporting Learning with Technology • Embedding Learning Technology • Developing Professional Practice • Developing Leaders	• Responding to Change in Higher Education • Staff and Educational Development • Leading Staff and Educational Development • Mentoring and Coaching

In this way the individual's learning is supported using a familiar cycle of learning and reflection drawing on Kolb's reflective process (1984) and the experiential, practitioner focus of learning from experience articulated by Boud, Keogh and Walker (1985). This structures steps by which a professional development need is identified, action taken, and the means to achieve it provided through an award. It includes reflection on progress and review leading to further development. In each case, individual awards provide targeted and specific outcomes to focus the learning of the practitioner around a particular function, area of practice or career stage. In this way, the organisation can use the awards to support specific learning around a role, a function or a stage in the career, developing expertise within the practitioner. As we show above, the awards themselves can be grouped to provide staged development for particular professional groups, an area of activity, or a role. This provides a tool that is practice-based and responsive in both organisational and individual learning terms, and one that promotes critical professionalism.

The process of recognition for an organisation seeking to adopt SEDA's professional development framework reinforces the organisation's own contribution to organisational learning. In the process of applying for recognition the organisation has to articulate how it develops and supports continuing professional development, explaining how this is situated within the organisational context, structure and strategy. The organisation is required to identify the particular awards it wishes to use and the ways that they will be supported and learning evidenced. In this way, the award integrates ideas for learning organisations and educational practitioner learning, providing a valuable resource for facilitators and human resource managers seeking to develop organisational spaces.

The awards do not need to be attached to formal courses as they can be delivered as a series of workshops or a programme of development. Therefore, where an institution has been recognised by SEDA, individual practitioners completing the continuing professional development activity receive national certification adding to their professional capital whilst providing evidence for the organisation of the quality of staff. The objective for gaining an award is for the development cycle to be evidenced and the values engaged with and applied. The SEDA professional development framework provides a creative tool through which organisational learning space can be designed and audited. It is a model that has been applied to developing our masters in education professional practice award.

Example 6: Using SEDA's professional development framework to structure a progression framework

The MEd was prompted by SEDA's professional development framework to design individual masters modules and course around roles and educational processes using the SEDA awards. Other SEDA-recognised institutions have made use of groups of awards and individual awards to support the development of professionalism for administrative and support staff and for technical staff, around new initiatives such as employability and other change agendas.

Up to now, this chapter has discussed critical professional development from an individual perspective and the wider national enablers an organisation can use. The next section proposes a way for organisations to respond to these influencing factors, combining the components into a single approach for enabling structures and learning space at organisational level.

The SCORED model

Here we consider how organisations might bring together all the elements and spaces within our model for critical professional development. It applies directly the assumptions that professional learning is socially constructed, that it requires targeted and critical reflection and that professionals learn best in activity that occurs in and around practice. We have termed it the SCORED model because it assumes those engaged in teaching and learning need:

- Space for reflection on practice;
- Communities of practice to learn from others;
- Opportunities that are structured for discussion and the sharing of good practice;
- Research and scholarship in learning and teaching;
- Education through formal courses;
- Development of critical professional perspectives.

This applies everything we have discussed as options for enabling structures and learning spaces, and the aspects of critical professionalism that underpin our model in Chapter Two. These elements can be enabled through organisational structures, within subjects and teams, through local and wider communities, as well as in networks. We will illustrate the SCORED model using the hypothetical case study of the Dewey Educational Institution.

Example 7: The SCORED model
Dewey Educational Institution is organised in schools around disciplinary groups providing a wide range of vocational, professional and academic subjects at foundation and degree level. The SCORED model has been applied through the use of institution-wide structures such as formal initial education, continuing professional development teaching courses, and a human resource system of workshops, some of which are

compulsory, some of which are provided to develop specific managerial processes and activities. These include learning technologies, mentoring and coaching or stress management, interview and appraisal activity. Alongside these initiatives, practitioners across the institution are supported using a teaching and learning forum which has regular meetings, a journal and magazine, and a virtual environment for members and also supports events and sponsors project activity. In this forum colleagues across all areas can come together and share practice ideas. There is also a mentoring and coaching network and a system of coaching that supports individuals through dialogue at key stages and levels of their career.

This institution-wide group and network is replicated at school level so that within schools and subjects sharing and exchange can take place. Meeting time forms part of the annual calendar, with small pots of funding and local champions providing support. Peer review of teaching is applied across Dewey Educational Institution and is structured around buddy teams using a process model, so review is not part of one-off contact but framed around curriculum design, delivery and review, so meetings occur regularly to discuss course, programme and teaching activity throughout the year.

Time is set aside for annual review of courses when teaching slows down over the summer to ensure that reflective development days for teams can take place and enhancement can be supported. Teams generally continue the dialogue naturally because the culture has fostered trust and shared ownership of practice. Within appraisal, time and actions are allocated and reviewed for individuals to take forward their professional development. Learning is supported through local allocation of funding for conferences, events and training, and the institution also has a programme of fellowships that support celebration and recognition of work by its employees. Students are drawn into this dialogic process using local 'discussion days' where teaching and learning matters are made the focus of reflection and exchange.

The example above suggests how, in an ideal world, the learning spaces can be structured into an organisation calendar and within school-based operations. The practice of education at Dewey is the subject of active investment of space and time. Processes have been formalised to ensure reflective space is allocated, and projects, networking and self-development have been resourced to reflect the importance of these activities for professional learning. For our hypothetical institution this does not necessarily mean everyone is equally engaged and is a critical professional, but there is a minimum expectation of engagement at team and programme level within schools that means everyone is drawn into an annual and embedded process of reflective planning, action and review.

One of the factors that the example above emphasises is dialogue at team and individual levels. We mention how Dewey Educational Institution uses mentoring, buddy schemes and team dialogue to enhance professional learning. In this respect it has taken and developed the ideas we discuss at the start of this chapter with respect to the individual drivers around professional learning. Figure 8.2 brings all these approaches together and suggests five steps by which Dewey Educational Institution has 'scored' in creating a culture that can support critical professional learning and sustain it through targeted work practices. Each step refers to a mechanism whereby Dewey Educational Institution has promoted and embedded principles of professional learning within enabling structures and learning spaces in order to develop the professional capital of workforce as critical professionals.

The use of champions, courses and consultation opportunities means that staff and students are able to engage with strategic and wider influences as well as the local teaching and learning experience. We observe that this mix of organisational embedding is actually quite widespread but lacks coherence and targeted application at strategic and operational levels in most organisations. What is absolutely imperative within the embedding of such organisation-wide approaches is that management, strategy, operational processes and individuals are all engaged. To achieve this level of embedding, strategies and management must recognise the importance and strategic value of an effective critically professional workforce and the value of professional capital as a concept that requires coherent, organisational investment. It requires the fundamental acceptance by managers and strategic leads that professional learning is worth the time and space we identify here. It also requires trust from employees that the approach is not solely about business efficiency, nor is it functionalist or technicist, but is about enabling, collaboration and enhance-

Figure 8.2 Five steps to organisational learning spaces and enabling structures using SCORED

1	**Practitioner-based activity, e.g.** • Practice-led and practice-based • Peer observation, course development and review, peer discussion; team learning and reflection
2	**Communities of Practice (CoP), e.g.** • Communities of Practice at local, team and department level • Community of 'champions' • Cross-institution networks, e.g. forums, groups and networks
3	**Practitioner Dialogue, e.g.** • Mentoring, buddy pairings, learning sets, peer review • Practitioner-based conversations
4	**Courses, e.g.** • Initial teacher training programmes • Continuing Professional Development courses and awards structured as a progression • Provide academic credibility and transferable
5	**Project activity, scholarship and research** • Action research and Scholarship of Teaching & Learning (SoTL) • Communities, journals, events for sharing outcomes

ment. In other words, it becomes what Fuller and Unwin (2004) call expansive learning, what Fraser *et al.* (2007) term 'transformative', and it has the potential for attaining what Evans (2010) terms 'extended professionalism'.

The role of the facilitator in critical professionalism

We suggested at the start of this chapter that it is important for the learning spaces and enabling structures of our model to be informed by deliberative and critical reflection. The concept of criticality we work with is based on interrogation of the practitioners' own assumptions and values, engagement with the wider context through interrogation of policy and strategic imperatives in relation to practice. This, we believe, supports the development of agency and awareness of the individual's own professional capital as an active responsibility and product of self-development. Critical professionalism also requires an understanding of choices and opportunities and knowing how to exploit them within the context of professional learning and organisational processes. To be effective this requires facilitation. The discussion of dialogue, outlined above, is one key way for this to take place.

In Chapter One, criticality was identified as requiring scholarship and engagement with processes of meta- cognition or meta-reflection (Van Manen, 1991; Hatton and Smith, 1995). If we draw on models of learning, the step of engaging at meta-levels of learning requires standing back and reflecting on reflection, or thinking about the process of one's own learning. Models are useful tools in this activity as they aid conceptualisation and the deconstruction of process, often making the abstract concrete. In our discussion of critical professionalism it has, therefore, been important to provide a definition for educational practitioners themselves to refer to and for those who are facilitating professional learning to apply.

An appreciation of the meaning and conceptualisation for professionalism proposed by our definition has to be understood and engaged with by stakeholders within the organisation. This is especially so for those who are involved in designing, structuring and implementing our model for critical professional development. Stakeholders in this process include:

- directors, vice chancellors and strategy developers;
- managers – in particular line, team or department managers;
- human resource workers and designers;
- initial teacher trainers, educational and academic developers;
- members of staff acting as champions, leads and co-ordinators for teams and developmental groups;
- mentors, coaches;
- all staff involved, including in peer review-type activity, for example.

Without understanding the concept of critical professionalism at this stakeholder level, it is unlikely that the application of our model will go beyond superficial implementation within the organisation. The result of this is isolated and short-term impact. In this situation, the impact of interventions will result in non-engagement, further frustrating practitioners' sense of their own value and worth to the organisation, damaging their professional capital. Interventions, even if well-meant, will be seen as additional to the workload or an audit control, rather than as an enhancing and valuable component for development. For those directly involved in implementation it is important that they appreciate the significance of critical professionalism expressed in our model, as they will be structuring and supporting the deliberative dialogic process and meta-processes for the individual practitioners. It is appropriate for stakeholders to consider their role and influence within organisational terms, and we summarise some key points relevant to this in Table 8.2 to clarify how their influence and role may contribute to effective implementation. In each case we identify the group, the role with respect to learning spaces and structures design, and key elements of the activity and stakeholder influence.

Stakeholders are not just designing spaces and structures, though we hope they do; it is more importantly about explicit direction and application of the model implying enactment that is both literal and discursive. Our discussion of reflection and professional learning in Chapters One and Two shows that the learning process requires

Table 8.2 Stakeholder roles and influence in applying a model for critical professional development

Stakeholder group	Role	Influence and activity, e.g.
Directors, vice chancellors and strategy developers	Setting culture	Strategic- learning and teaching, human resource; discussion consultation, planning and resourcing; culture, agenda-setting and accountability
Managers, line managers	Setting context, designing	Design, appraisal, planning; interpretation and operationalising; setting actions, identifying opportunities, monitoring
Human resources	Setting context, designing, enabling	Structuring, designing, planning and operationalising, monitoring
Teacher trainers, developers	Designing and enabling	Course, workshop, process design; facilitation, education and support; modelling practice
Champions, leads and co-ordinators	Designing and enabling	Process facilitation, support; motivation and modelling practice
Mentors, etc	Enabling	Enabling, dialogic support; interpretation, operationalising

structure, process and direction. Acceptance of the central concept of critical professionalism requires spaces to be designed within processes and workplace activity that have delegated time, resources and physical and procedural space. Effective implementation also requires direct and specific engagement in dialogue to establish shared understanding of the model. Dialogue needs to cover aspects of strategy, operation, planning, resourcing, and the implications of critical professionalism and professional capital for all parties.

Through the examples in this chapter, and our earlier case studies, we offer concrete and practical ideas for how an organisation can utilise the concept of critical professionalism in constructing learning spaces and enabling structures for professionals within its systems and processes. In this chapter, we have deconstructed our model to show how the inner and outer circles can contribute to the organisational aspect of the process. This reinforces the significance of the interrelationship between wider contexts and the complex practice setting including the role and relevance of professional capital, agency and choice in creating a critical professional workforce. Another significant part of the relationship is how individual education professionals learn. The organisational level is where these two elements are combined within the spaces and structures created for professional learning.

Within an increasingly supercomplex educational context, organisations can only succeed in engaging the workforce if they apply a learning approach that supports the enabling of critical professional engagement. If professional engagement and learning is left solely to the individual practitioner it will become impossible to implement unilaterally: practitioners will increasingly be left with neither the time, the resource, nor the inclination as workloads, demands and expectations grow. Our experience has shown what is possible in working with individuals, organisations and linking this to the wider context. Our model, developed from this experience identifies approaches, founded on theory and practical application, which we hope will support the critical professional development of many others in education.

References

Anderson, L. W. and Krathwohl, D. R. (2001) (eds.) *A Taxonomy for Learning, Teaching and Assessing: A Review of Bloom's Taxonomy of Educational Objectives.* Complete editions, New York: Longman.

Appleby, Y. (2009) '"It's just like being a student": Making space for teachers to think', *International Journal of Learning*, 16: 11, 23–24.

Appleby, Y. and Banks, C. (2009) (eds.) *Looking Back and Moving Forward: Reflecting on our Practice as Teacher Educators.* Preston: University of Central Lancashire.

Appleby, Y. and Barton, A. (2012) 'Case study: engaging conceptual learning about threshold concepts with pots and pans', *Journal of Learning Development in Higher Education*, 4.

Appleby, Y. and Hiller, Y. (2011) 'Exploring practice–research networks for critical professional learning', *Studies in Continuing Education*, 36: 1, 1–13.

Argyris, C. and Schon, D. (1995) *Organisational Learning II Theory Method and Practice.* Reading, MA: Addison Wesley.

Atherton, M. and Barnes, L. (2012) 'Deaf people as British Sign Language teachers: experiences and aspirations', *Deafness & Education International*, 14: 4 (December 2012), 184–198.

Avis, J. (2010) 'Workplace learning, knowledge, practice and transformation', *Journal for Critical Policy Studies*, 8: 2, 165–193.

Ball, S. (2003) 'The teachers' soul and the terrors of performativity', *Journal of Education Policy*, 18: 2, 215–228.

Ball, S. (2006) *Education Policy and Social Class.* Abingdon: Routledge.

Ball, S. (2008) *The Education Debate*, Bristol: Policy Press.

Barnes, L. and Doe, L. (2007) 'Language Tutors under the microscope', in L. Barnes, F. J. Harrington, J. Williams and M. Atherton (eds.), *Deaf Students in Higher Education: current research and practice.* Coleford: Douglas McLean, 104–117.

Barnes, L. and Eichmann, H. (2010) 'No time? No support? No idea?: The Future of BSL Teaching'. University of Central Lancashire (Unpublished Research Report).

Barnes, L. and Padden, T. (2009) 'Researching the Pedagogic Needs of BSL Teachers'. University of Central Lancashire (Unpublished Research Report).

Barnett, R. (2008) 'Critical professionalism in an age of supercomplexity', in B. Cunningham (ed.), *Exploring Professionalism*. London: Bedford Way Papers, Institute of Education, 190–209.

Barnett, R. and Coate, K. (2005) *Engaging the Curriculum in HE*. Maidenhead: SRHE/OUP.

Barnett, R., Parry, G. and Coate, K. (2001) 'Conceptualising Curriculum Change', *Teaching in HE*, 6: 4, 435–449.

Bathmaker, A. and Avis, J. (2005) 'Becoming a lecturer in further education in England; the construction of professional identity and the role of communities of practice', *Journal of Education for Teaching: International Research and Pedagogy*, 31: 1, 47–62.

Bathmaker, A. and Avis, J. (2007) '"How do I cope with that?" The challenge of "schooling" cultures in further education for trainee FE lecturers', *British Educational Research Journal*, 33: 4, 509–532.

Becher, T. and Trowler, P. (2001) *Academic Tribes and Territories*. Buckingham: SRHE/OUP.

Beijaard, D., Meijer, P. and Verloop, N. (2004) 'Reconsidering research on teachers professional identity', *Teaching and Teacher Education*, 20, 107–128.

Bell, M. (2001) 'Supported Reflective Practice: a programme of peer observation and feedback for academic teaching development', *International Journal for Academic Development*, 6: 1, 29–39.

Billett, S. (2002) 'Critiquing Workplace Learning Discourse: Participation and Continuity at Work', *Studies in the Education of Adults*, 34: 1, 56–67.

Billett, S. (2004) 'Learning through work: Workplace participatory practices', in H. Rainbird, A. Fuller and A. Munro (eds.), *Workplace Learning in Context*. London: Routledge, 109–125.

Bleakley, A., Farrow R., Gould, D. and Marshall, R. (2003) 'Learning how to see doctors making judgments in the visual domain', Paper presented at third International Conference on Research, Work and Learning, Tampere, Finland, July, in Robson, J. (2006) *Teacher Professionalism in Further and Higher Education Challenges to Culture and Practice*. London: Routledge.

Bloom, B. S., Engelhart, M. D., Furst, E. J., Hill, W. H. and Krathwohl, D. R. (1956) *Taxonomy of Educational Objectives: The Classification of Educational Goals; Handbook I: Cognitive Domain* New York, Longmans, Green.

Boud, D. (1999) 'Situating academic development in professional work: Using peer learning' *International Journal for Academic Development*, 4: 1, 3–10.

Boud, D. (2010) 'Relocating reflection in the context of practice', in H. Bradbury, N. Frost, S. Kilminster and M. Zukas (eds.), *Beyond Reflective Practice: New approaches to professional lifelong learning*. London: Routledge, 25–36.

Boud, D. and Falchikov, N. (2007) (eds.) *Rethinking Assessment in Higher Education Learning for the longer term*. Abingdon: Routledge.

Boud, D. and Walker, D.(1990) 'Making the most of experience', *Studies in Continuing Education*, 12: 2, 61–80.

Boud, D., Keogh, R. and Walker, D. (eds.) (1985) *Reflection: Turning Experience into Learning*. London: Kogan Page.

Bourdieu, P. (1989) *Language and Symbolic Power*. Cambridge: Polity Press.

Bourdieu, P. (1998) *Acts of Resistance: Against the Tyranny of the Market*. New York: The New Press.

Boyer, E. L. (1990) *Scholarship Reconsidered*. San Francisco, CA: Carnegie Foundation and Jossey-Bass.

Brew, A. (2010) 'Transforming academic practice through scholarship', *International Journal for Academic Development*, 15: 2, 105–116.

Brockbank, A. and McGill, I. (1998) *Facilitating Reflective Learning in Higher Education*, Buckingham: SRHE/OUP.

Brookfield, S. (1995) *Becoming a Critically Reflective Teacher*. San Francisco: Jossey-Bass.

Children Act, 2004 [Online]. Available at: www.opsi.gov.uk/acts/acts2004/ukpga_20040031_en_1 (Accessed 18 April 2013).

Clughen, L. and Hardy, C. (2011) 'Creating participatory writing cultures in UK Higher Education', *Journal of Academic Writing*, 1: 1, 71–78.

Colley, H., James, D. and Dinet, K. (2007) 'Unbecoming teachers: towards a more dynamic notion of professional participation', *Journal of Educational Policy*, 22: 2, 173–193.

Cousin, G. (2006) 'An introduction to threshold concepts', *Planet*, 17, 4–5.

Cousin, G. (2010) 'Neither teacher-centered not student centered: threshold concepts and research partnerships', *Journal of Learning Development in Higher Education*, 2, 1–9.

Cox, S. and King, D. (2006) 'Skills set: an approach to embed employability in course design', *Education and Training*, 48: 4, 262–274.

Crook, D. (2008) 'Some historical perspectives on professionalism', in B. Cunningham (ed.), *Exploring Professionalism*. London: Bedford Way Papers, Institute of Education, 10–28.

Cunningham, B. (ed.) (2008) *Exploring Professionalism*. London: Bedford Way Papers, Institute of Education.

CWDC (Children's Workforce Development Council) (2010) *The Common Core of Skills and Knowledge*. CDWW.

Davies, L. (2000) '"Why kick the L out of Learning?" The development of students' employability skills through part-time working', *Education and Training*, 42: 8, 436–444.

Davies, L. (2004) *Education and Conflict: Complexity and Chaos*. London: Routledge Falmer.

Davies, S., Swinburne, D. and Williams, G. (2006) *Writing Matters*. London: The Royal Literary Fund.

Day, C. (1999) 'Developing Teachers: the challenges of lifelong learning', in Evans, L. (2008) 'Professionalism, Professionality and the Development of Education Professionals', *British Journal of Education Studies*, 56: 1, 20–38.

Department for Business, Innovation and Skills (2010) *Skills for Sustainable Growth*. URN 10/ 274, London: HMSO.

Department for Business, Innovation and Skills (2011) *New Challenges, New Chances*. URN 11/1380, London: HMSO.

Department for Business, Innovation and Skills (2012a) *Evaluation of FE Teachers Qualifications (England) Regulations 2007*. BIS Research Report, No. 66, London: HMSO.

Department for Business, Innovation and Skills (2012b) *Professionalism in Further Education, Interim Report of the Independent Review Panel, March 2012*. URN 12/670, London: HMSO.

Department for Business, Innovation and Skills (2012c) *Consultation on Revocation of the Further Education Workforce Regulations, Government Response, August 2012*. URN 12/970, London: HMSO.

Department for Business, Innovation and Skills (2012d) *Professionalism in Further Education, Final Report of the Independent Review Panel, October 2012*. URN 12/1198, London: HMSO.

Department for Education (2003) *Every Child Matters, Green Paper*. Norwich: The Stationery Office. (CM 5860).

Department for Education and Skills (2005) *Common Core of Skills and Knowledge for the Children's Workforce*. Nottingham: DfES http://webarchive.national archives.gov.uk/20100202100434/dcsf.gov.uk/everychildmatters/strategy/ deliveringservices1/commoncore/commoncoreofskillsandknowledge/ (Accessed: 18 April 2013).

Department of Health and Home Office (2003) *The Victoria Climbié Inquiry*, Norwich: The Stationery Office.

Dewey, J. (1938) *Experience and Education*. New York: Collier.

DEX (Deaf Ex-Mainstreamers Group) (2003) (eds.) *Between a Rock and a Hard Place*. Wakefield: DEX.

Doncaster, K. and Thorne, L. (2000) 'Reflection and planning: Essential elements of professional doctorate', *Reflective Practice*, 1: 3, 391–399.

Doyle, M. and Griffin, M. (2012) 'Raised aspirations and attainment? A review of the impact of Aimhigher (2004–2011) on widening participation in higher education in England', *London Review of Education*, 10: 1, 75–88.

Drake, P. with Heath, L. (2011) *Practitioner Research at Doctoral Level: Developing coherent research methodologies.* Abingdon: Routledge.

Dreyfus, H. and Dreyfus, S. (1986) *Mind over Machine: The Power of Human Intuition and Expertise in the Era of The Computer.* Oxford: Blackwell.

Eisner, E. (1985) *The Educational Imagination.* New York: Macmillan.

Emery, S. (2007) 'The loneliness of the long-distance post-graduate student', in L. Barnes, F. J. Harrington, J. Williams and M. Atherton (eds.), *Deaf Students in Higher Education: Current research and practice.* Coleford: Douglas McLean.

Ennis, R. (2011) 'The Nature of Critical Thinking: An Outline of Critical Thinking Dispositions and Abilities', revised version of a presentation at the Sixth International Conference on Thinking. MIT, Cambridge, MA, July, 1994 [Online]. Available at: http://faculty.education.illinois.edu/rhennis/documents/TheNatureofCriticalThinking_51711_000.pdf. Accessed: 18 April 2013.

Eraut, M. (1994) *Developing Professional Knowledge and Competence.* Abingdon: Falmer Press.

Eraut, M. (2000) 'Non-formal learning and tacit knowledge in professional work', *British Journal of Educational Psychology,* 70:1, 113–136.

Eraut, M. (2004) 'Informal Learning in the workplace', *Studies in Continuing Education,* 26:2, 247–273.

Evans, L. (2008) 'Professionalism, Professionality and the Development of Education Professionals', *British Journal of Educational Studies,* 56: 1, 28–38.

Evans, L. (2010) 'Developing the European researcher: 'extended' professionality within the Bologna Process', *Professional Development in Education,* 36: 4, 1–15.

Excellence Gateway: www.excellencegateway.org.uk/node/64.

Excellence Gateway BSL teachers' network: www.excellencegateway.org.uk/node/17997.

Excellence Gateway BSL teachers' resources: www.excellencegateway.org.uk/bslteachers.

Fallows, S. and Steven, C. (2000) 'Building employability skills into higher education curriculum: a university wide initiative', *Education and Training,* 42: 2, 75–82.

Fell, T., Flint, K. and Haines, I. (2011) *Professional Doctorates in the UK.* UKCGE.

Fenwick, T. (2009) 'Made to measure? Reconsidering assessment in professional continuing education', *Studies in Continuing Education,* 31: 3, 229–244.

Fenwick, T. and Farrell, L. (eds.) (2012) *Knowledge, Mobilization and Educational Research: Politics, Languages and Responsibilities.* London: Routledge.

Fichtman, N. and Yendol Hoppey, D. (2008) *The Reflective Educator's Guide to Professional Development: Coaching Inquiry-Oriented Learning Communities.* London: Corwin Press, Sage Publications.

Field, J. (2008) *Social Capital* (2nd edition). London: Routledge.

Finn, P. (2011) 'Critical thinking: Knowledge and skills for evidence-based practice', *Language Speech and Hearing Services in Schools*, 42, 69–72.

Forehand, M. (2001) 'Bloom's Taxonomy', in M. Orey (ed.), *Emerging Perspectives on Learning, Teaching, and Technology*, [Online] Available at: http://projects.coe. uga.edu/epltt/ (Accessed: 18 April 2013).

Foster, A. (2005) *14–19 Curriculum Qualifications Reform: Final Report on Working Group on 14–19 Reform*. London: HMSO.

Fraser, C., Kennedy, A., Reid, L. and McKinney, S. (2007) 'Teachers' continuing professional development: Contested concepts, understandings and models', *Journal of In-service Education*, 33: 2, 153–169.

Freire, P. (1972) *Pedagogy of the Oppressed*. New York: Herder and Herder.

Fuller, F. (1970) 'Personalised education for teachers: one application of the teacher concerns model. Austin, Texas: University of Texas', in M. Eraut (1994) *Developing Professional Knowledge and Competence*. Abingdon: The Falmer Press, 72.

Fuller, A. and Unwin, L. (2004) 'Expansive learning environments: integrating organizational and personal development', in H. Rainbird, A. Fuller and A. Munro (eds.), *Workplace Learning in Context*. London: Routledge, 126–145.

Ganobcsik–Williams, L. (2004) *A report on the Teaching of Academic Writing in UK Higher Education*. London: The Royal Literary Fund.

Ghaye, A. and Ghaye, K. (1998) *Teaching and Learning through Critical Reflective Practice*. Abingdon: David Fulton.

Ghaye, A., Melander-Wikman, A., Kisare, M., Chambers, P., Bergmark, U., Kostenius, C. and Lillyman, S. (2008) 'Participatory and appreciative action and reflection PAAR – democratizing reflective practices', *Reflective Practice*, 9: 4, 361–397.

Gibbons, M., Limoges, C., Nowotny, H., Schwartzman, S., Scott, P. and Trow, M. (1994) *The New Production of Knowledge. The Dynamics of Science and Research in Contemporary Societies*. London: Sage.

Giroux, H., Lankshear, C., McLaren, P., Peters, M. (1996) *Counternarratives: Cultural Studies and Critical Pedagogies in Postmodern Spaces*. London: Routledge.

Gregorc, A. (1973) 'Developing plans for professional growth', *NASSP Bulletin* December 1973, 1–8, p. 63, in Moon, J. (1999) *Reflection in learning and Professional Development: Theory and Practice*. London: Routledge Falmer.

Grossman, P. G., Hammermas, K. and McDonald, E. (2009) 'Redefining teaching, reimagining teacher education', *Teachers and Teaching: Theory and Practice*, 15: 2, 273–289.

Groundwater-Smith, S. and Sachs, J. (2002) 'The activist professional and the reinstatement of trust', *Cambridge Journal of Education*, 32: 3, 341.

Guile, D. and Lucas, N. (1999) 'Rethinking initial teacher education and professional development in FE: towards the learning professional', in A. Green and N. Lucas (eds.), *Further Education and Lifelong Learning: Realigning the Sector for the Twenty First Century*. London: Bedford Way Papers, Institute of Education.

Habermas, J. (1974) *Theory and Practice*. London: Heinemann.

Haigh, N. (2005) 'Everyday conversation as a context for professional learning and development international', *International Journal of Academic Development*, 10: 1, 3–16.

Harrington, F. J. and Turner, G.H. (2001) *Interpreting Interpreting*. Coleford: Douglas McLean.

Hatton, N. and Smith, D. (1995) 'Reflection in Teacher Education: towards Definition and Implementation', *Teaching & Teacher Education*, 11: 1, 33–49.

Healey, M. (2001) *The Scholarship of Teaching in HE: An Evolving Idea*. York: The HE Academy.

Healey, M. and Jackson, B. (2004) 'Pedagogic research and reflection in CETLs bids', [Online]. HEFCE. Available from: www.hefce.ac.uk/learning/tinits/CETL/devtday/ Accessed 21 June 2010.

Heron, J. (1999) *The Complete Facilitator's Handbook*. London: Kogan Page.

Hessmann, J. and Pyfers, L. (2013) 'BSL as a second language for deaf sign language users: Insights from the Signs2Go online course', in D. McKee, R. S. Rosen and R. McKee (eds.), *Teaching and Learning of Signed Languages: International Perspectives and Practices*. Basingstoke: Palgrave Macmillan (in press).

Hillier, Y. (2006) *Everything You Need to Know About FE Policy*. London: Continuum.

Hillier, Y. and Appleby, Y. (2012) 'Supporting professionalism: See-saw politics and the paradox of deregulation', *Adults Learning*, Winter, 2012, 24: 2, 8–12.

Ho, A. (2000). 'A conceptual change approach to staff development: a model for professional design', *International Journal of Academic Development*, 5: 1, 30–41.

hooks, b. (1994) *Teaching to Transgress: Education as the Practice of Freedom*. London: Routledge.

Hughes, W. (2000) *Critical Thinking*. London: Broadview Press.

I-Sign Project (2009) www.i-sign.org.uk/home/.

Illeris, K. (2002) *The Three Dimensions of Learning: Contemporary Learning Theory in the Tension Field Between the Cognitive, the Emotional and the Social*. Roskilde: Roskilde University Press.

Illeris K. (ed.) (2009) *Contemporary Theories of Learning; Learning Theorists in their own Words*. Abingdon: Routledge.

James, D. and Biesta, G. (2007) *Improving Learning Cultures in Further Education*. Abingdon: Routledge.

Jenkins, A. and Healey, M. (2005) Institutional Strategies to link Teaching and Research. York: Higher Education Academy.

Kahn, P., Wareham, T., Young, R., Willis, I. and Pilkington, R. (2008) 'Exploring a practitioner-based interpretive approach to reviewing research literature',

International Journal of Research and Method in Education, 31: 2, 169–180.

Kahn, P., Young, R., Grace, S., Pilkington, R., Rush, L., Tomkinson, B., Willis, I. (2006) *The Role and Effectiveness of Reflective Practices in Programmes for New Academic Staff: A Grounded Practitioner Review of the Research Literature.* University of Manchester: Higher Education Academy.

Kahn, P., Young, R., Grace, S., Pilkington, R., Rush, L., Tomkinson, B. and Willis, I. (2009) 'Theory and legitimacy in professional education: a practitioner review of reflective processes within programmes for new academic staff', *International Journal for Academic Development*, 13: 3, 161–173.

Kang, M. and Glassman, M. (2010) 'Moral action as social capital, moral thought as cultural capital', *Journal of Moral Education*, 39: 1, 21–36.

Knight, P., Tait, J. and Yorke, M. (2006) 'The professional learning of teachers in HE', *Studies in HE*, 31: 3, 319–339.

Kolb, D. (1984) *Experiential Learning.* Englewood Cliffs, NJ: Prentice Hall.

Kreber, C. (2004) 'An analysis of two models of reflection and their implications for educational development', *International Journal of Academic Development*, 9: 1, 29–49.

Kreber, C., Klampfleitner, M., McCune, V., Bayne, S. and Knottenbelt, M. (2009) 'What do you mean by "Authentic"? A comparative review of the literature on conceptions of authenticity in teaching', *Adult Education Quarterly*, 58: 1, 22–43.

Larrivee, B. (2008) 'Development of a tool to assess teachers' level of reflective practice', *Reflective Practice*, 9: 3, 341–360.

Laurillard, D. A. (1999) 'Conversational framework for individual learning applied to the "Learning Organisation" and the "Learning Society"', *Systems Research and Behavioural Science*, 16, 113–122.

Lave, J. and Wenger, E. (1991) 'Legitimate peripheral participation in communities of practice', in R. Harrison, F. Reeve, A. Hanson and J. Clarke (eds.) (2002), *Supporting Lifelong Learning 1 Perspectives on Learning.* London: OUP/Routledge, 111–126.

Ligorio, M. and Cesar, M. (eds.) (2013) *Interplays between Dialogical Learning and Dialogical Self.* USA: IAP.

Lindkvist, L. (2005) 'Knowledge communities and knowledge collectivities: A typology of knowledge work in groups', *Journal of Management Studies*, 42: 6, 189–210.

Lucas, N., Nasta, T. and Rogers, L. (2012) 'From fragmentation to chaos? The regulation of initial teacher training in further education', *British Educational Research Journal*, 38: 4, 677–695.

Lyle, E. (2012) 'Learning organisation(al) learning', *International Journal of Business and Social Science* Special Issue, 3: 6, 217–221.

Macdonald, R. and Wisdom, J. (eds.) (2002) *Academic and Educational Development Research Evaluation and Changing Practice in HE.* London: Kogan Page.

MacKinnon, M. (2001) 'Using observation feedback to promote academic development', *International Journal for Academic Development*, 6: 1, 21–28.

Magna Charta Universitatum. Retrieved May 2013 from www.magna-charta. org/library/userfiles/file/mc_english.pdf

Manouchehri, A. (2002) 'Developing teaching knowledge through peer discourse', *Teaching and Teacher Education*, 18, 715–737.

Martin, W. (2005) 'Education as dialogue: some implications for deaf learners', Supporting Deaf People (SDP3) online conference, Direct Learn Services Ltd., www.online-conference.co.uk/WebX?14@43.uQVmaG8daGw.39364@ ee8424.

Meyer, J. and Land, R. (2003) 'Threshold concepts and troublesome knowledge: Linkages to ways of thinking and practising within the disciplines', *Enhancing Teaching and Learning Environments*, Occasional Report 4.

Meyer, J. and Land, R. (2005) 'Threshold concepts and troublesome knowledge (2): Epistemological considerations and a conceptual framework for teaching and learning', *Higher Education*, 49: 3, 373–388.

Mole, J. and Peacock, D. (2006) 'Language issues for deaf students in Higher Education', in M. Adams and S. Brown (eds.), *Towards Inclusive Learning in HE: Developing Curricula for Disabled Students*. London: Routledge.

Moon, J. A. (1999) *Reflection in Learning and Professional Development: Theory and Practice*. Abingdon: Routledge Falmer.

Moore, A. and Ash, A. (2002) Reflective practice in beginning teachers: Helps, hindrances and the role of the critical other, www.leeds.ac.uk/educol/ documents/0000253.htm

Moore, S. (2003) 'Writers' retreats for academics: exploring and increasing motivation to write', *Journal of Further and Higher Education*, 27: 3, 333–342.

Moreberg, S., Lagerstrom, M. and Dellve, L. (2011) 'The school nursing profession in relation to Bourdieu's concept of capital, habitus and field', *Scandinavian Journal of Caring Sciences*, 26, 355–362.

Morss, K. and Murray, R. (2001) 'Researching academic writing within a structures programme: Insights and outcomes', *Studies in Higher Education*, 26: 1, 35–52.

Murray, R. (2002) 'Writing development for lecturers moving from Further to Higher Education: A case study', *Journal of Further and Higher Education*, 26: 3, 229–239.

Murray, R., Stekley, L., Macleod, I. (2012) 'Research leadership in writing for publication: A theoretical framework', *British Educational Research Journal*, 38: 5, 765–786.

Murray, R., Thow, M., Moore, S. and Murphy, M. (2008) 'The writing consultation: developing academic writing practices', *Journal of Further and Higher Education*, 32: 2, 119–127.

National Deaf Children's Society (2008) *Must Do Better! Barriers to Achievement by Deaf Children*. London: National Deaf Children's Society.

Office for Standards in Education (2003) *The Initial Teacher Training of Further Education Teachers: A Survey. November, 2003*. HMI 1766, Crown Copyright, Ofsted Publication Centre.

Ozga, J. (2012) 'Knowledge stocks and flows: data and educational governance', in T. Fenwick and L. Farrell (eds.), *Knowledge Mobilization and Educational Research: Politics, Languages and Responsibilities*. London: Routledge, 73–86.

Paulson, E. (2011) 'Group communications and critical thinking competence development using a reality based project', *Business Communications Quarterly*, 74: 4, 400–411.

Pedler, M. (1996) *Action Learning for Managers*. London: The Learning Company Project.

Pedler, M., Burgoyne, J. and Boydell, T. (1996) *The Learning Company: A Strategy for Sustainable Development*. London: McGraw Hill.

Peel, D. (2005) 'Dual professionalism: Facing the challenges of continuing professional development in the workplace?' *Reflective Practice*, 6: 1, 123–140.

Pilkington, R. (2004) 'Using the SEDA PDF to frame organisational and professional development', *Educational Developments*, 5: 2, June 5–9.

Pilkington, R. (2006) 'Supporting lecturers to improve essay assessment', in C. Rust (ed.), *Improving Student Learning through Assessment: Proceedings of the 2005 13th International Symposium*. Oxford: OCSLD, pp.295–309.

Pilkington, R. (2011a) 'What about dialogue? An alternative assessment mechanism for professional learning', *Educational Developments*, 1: 2, 13–16.

Pilkington, R. (2011b) 'Using reflective dialogue to assess professional learning, (2010–11) The project website.' Retrieved January 7 2012 from www.escalate.ac.uk/6333.

Pilkington, R. (2013) 'Professional dialogues: exploring an alternative means of assessing the professional learning of experienced HE academics', *International Journal for Academic Development*, 18: 3, 251–263.

Pill, A. (2005) 'Models of professional development in the education and practice of new teachers in HE', *Teaching in HE*, 10: 2, 175–188.

Plowright, D. and Barr, G. (2012) 'An integrated professionalism in further education: a time for phronesis?', *Journal of Further and Higher Education*, 36: 1, 1–16.

Plymouth Safeguarding Board (2010) Serious Case Review Overview Report, Executive Summary in respect of Nursery Z, March 2010, [Online] Available at: www.plymouth.gov.uk/text/serious_case_review_nursery_z.pdf. Accessed: 18 April 2013.

Race, P. (2004) *The Lecturer's Toolkit*, 2nd Edition. London: Routledge Falmer.

Reynolds, M. and Vince, R. (2004) *Organizing Reflection*. Aldershot: Gower.

Roberts, J. (2006) 'Limits to communities of practice', *Journal of Management Studies*, 43: 3, 623–639.

Robson, J. (2006) *Teacher Professionalism in Further and Higher Education Challenges to Culture and Practice*. London: Routledge.

Rodda, M. and Eleweke, J. (2000) 'Theories of literacy development in deaf people with limited English proficiency', *Deafness and Education International*, 2: 2, 101–113.

Sachs, J. (2000) 'The activist profession', *International Journal of Educational Change*, 1: 1, 77–79.

Sachs, J. (2001) 'Teacher professional identity: competing discourses, competing outcomes', *Journal of Educational Policy*, 16: 2, 149–16.

Schon, D. (1983) *The Reflective Practitioner*. New York, USA: Basic Books (Reprint, 2009) Ashgate Publishing.

Schon, D. (1987) *Educating the Reflective Practitioner*. San Francisco: Jossey Bass,

Scott, D., Brown, A., Lunt, I. and Thorne, L. (2004) *Professional Doctorates: integrating professional and Academic Knowledge*. Maidenhead: SRHE/ OUP.

Senge, P. (1990) *The Fifth Discipline: The Art and Practice of the Learning Organization*. New York: Doubleday.

Shulman, L. S. (1987) 'Knowledge and teaching: foundations of the New Reform', *Harvard Education Review*, 57: 1, 1–22.

Stefani, L. (ed.) (2011) *Evaluating the Effectiveness of Academic Development*. London: Routledge.

Stewart, A. (2009) *Continuing Your Professional Development in Lifelong Learning*. London: Continuum.

Stierer, B. and Antoniou, M. (2004) 'Are there distinctive methodologies for pedagogic research in higher education?', *Teaching in Higher Education*, 9: 3, 275–285.

The HE Academy (2006) *The UK Professional Standards Framework*. HEFCE, UUK.

The HE Academy (2011) *The UK Professional Standards Framework*. HEFCE, UUK.

Trevitt, A. C. F. and Perera, C. (2009) 'Self and continuous professional learning (development): Issues of curriculum and identity in developing academic practice', *Journal of Teaching in Higher Education*, 14: 4, 347–359.

Trigwell, K. (2001) 'Professionalism in practice: the role of research into higher education', Keynote address to the Annual Conference of the Institute for Learning and Teaching in Higher Education, York: United Kingdom.

University and College Union (2013) 'Towards a UCU Policy on Professionalism a paper for members', UCU. Accessed 17 April 2013 from www.ucu.org.uk/professionalism.

Van Manen, M. (1977) 'Linking ways of knowing with ways of being practical', *Curriculum Inquiry*, 6: 3, 205–28.

Van Manen, M. (1991) *The Tact of Teaching*. Albany: The State University of New York Press.

Vloet, K., Jacobs, G. and Veugeler, W. (2013) 'Dialogic learning in teachers' professional identities', in M. Ligorio, and M. Cesar (eds.), *Interplays between Dialogical Learning and Dialogical Self*. USA: IAP, 419–457.

Vygotsky, L. S. (1978) *Mind in Society*. Cambridge MA: Harvard University Press.

Watts, J. (2008) 'Challenges of supervising part-time PhD students: towards student-centred practice', *Teaching in HE*, 13: 3, 369–373.

Wellington, J. and Sikes, P. (2006) 'A doctorate in a tight compartment: why do students choose a professional doctorate and what impact does it have on their personal lives', *Studies in HE*, 31: 6, 160–176.

Wenger, E. and Snyder, W. (2000) 'Communities of practice: the organizational frontier', *Harvard Business Review*, Jan–Feb, 139–145.

Woolfe, T. (2004) 'Employment and Deaf people: Are we moving in the right direction?' Supporting Deaf People online conference. Retrieved from www.online-conference.net/sdp2004.htm.

Yorke, M. (2000) 'A cloistered virtue? Pedagogical research and policy in UK Higher Education', *Higher Education Quarterly*, 54, 106–26.

Zukas, M. And Malcolm, J. (2007) 'Learning from adult education', *Academy Exchange*, 6. York: The Higher Education Academy.

Index

Note: Page numbers in **bold** type refer to **figures**
Page numbers in *italic* type refer to *tables*